'Bryony's talents as both cook and photographer are clearly evident in this book. Her joie de vivre *is infectious and her recipes mouthwatering'*

ALAN TITCHMARSH MBE

'Here is a book, which can really make you feel both healthy and happy. Thanks to Bryony Hill's beautiful and evocative photographs and her intimate writing you can imagine yourself with Bryony in her wonderful garden about to eat one of her delicious dishes. Then when you read her advice and simple recipes you'll realise that even in a small garden you can create the idyll yourself'

JOSCELINE DIMBLEBY, COOKERY WRITER AND JOURNALIST

'I have had the pleasure of dining at Bryony's where everything was from her garden – fresh and delicious. She is an imaginative person and it is reflected in her cooking. I also cook every day, but lack her creative approach to food so I cannot wait to purchase her book. It will be a help to me, as she will include recipes for one, as I am hopeless at trying to adapt recipes for six. I can hardly wait'

JUDY PARFITT, ACTRESS (*CALL THE MIDWIFE*, *MIDSOMER MURDERS*, *JEWEL IN THE CROWN*, *GIRL WITH A PEARL EARRING*)

My mother taught me nearly everything I know to do with cooking and gardening. She had the greenest fingers, the largest heart and the warmest, most welcoming kitchen albeit chaotic in its untidiness. When it came to the sad task of sorting her affairs after she died I found her camera, still with a film inside. It took me six months to pluck up the courage to have it developed. Ma's tomatoes were legendary, as was the soup she made from them, and one of the photos made me laugh out loud, then cry. Her potato crop kept her going most of the year but her pride and joy was a variety of tomato called Marmande. That year they had grown so large, in order to prevent the branch from breaking whilst they continued to ripen, she had fished out one of her white lace bras and suspended it on the plant in order to support the biggest tomatoes I have ever seen in my life. She is a tough act to follow.

BRIDGET ALISON ROSEMARY JARVIS (1922-2007)

Bryony Hill

GROW *happy* COOK *happy* BE *happy*

From my garden to my kitchen

Published by RedDoor
www.reddoorpublishing.com

ISBN 978-1-910453-58-2

A CIP catalogue record for this book is available from the British Library

Cover design: Gemma Wilson
Design and typesetting: Gemma Wilson

Printed by Bell & Bain Ltd, Glasgow, UK

Notes and measurements

Metric, imperial and also metric cups are given for the recipes.
1 metric cup = 250ml
1¼ cups = 300ml
2½ cups = 600ml

All spoon measures are level unless specified.
1 tsp = 5ml spoon; 1 tbsp = 15ml spoon.

Always try to buy organic produce if possible.

Use semi-skimmed milk unless specified in the recipe.

Organic and free-range eggs are recommended. Use medium-sized eggs unless specified in the recipe.

If using citrus zest then try to buy fruit unwaxed. All fruit and vegetables should be thoroughly washed.

The oven should be preheated to the specified temperature. If using a fan-assisted oven, adjust the temperature accordingly.

Non-stick frying pans make life much easier.

Notes

To give you a helping hand, please note the following:

- slug = about 2 tbsp
- splosh = about 1 tbsp
- squirt or dash = about 1 tsp
- dollop = er, dollop

To save repeating myself, here are a few useful tips.

- If you are going to freeze a soup, sauce or other savoury dish it's best to avoid including garlic at the time of cooking as freezing might taint the flavour; add it when reheating.
- With regard to making jams and jellies start by putting a small metal dish or saucer in the freezer to chill, then in order to check it will set, drop a small amount of the jam or jelly on to the dish. If it wrinkles when you draw your finger through it, it's ready. To prevent preserves from going mouldy always sterilise your jars first either in a warm oven for 5 minutes or by filling them with boiling water and draining well.
- Many of my recipes include Swiss chard. I grow this every year partly because until recently it was almost impossible to buy since it has a short shelf life. It is a forgiving vegetable able to battle through the worst wind, frost and rain all year. Nowadays, thank goodness, it is available in good supermarkets along with Tuscan and other varieties of kale. However, if you are unable either to grow it yourself or don't find it in the shops spinach is a perfect alternative, but do bear in mind that spinach, unlike its more robust cousin, reduces considerably and you will have to adjust the quantities accordingly.

YOU CAN FIND
ME IN THE
Garden

PROLOGUE

A few days before Christmas in 2015 my husband, Jimmy, passed away after a long and brave battle with Alzheimer's disease. Thankfully I was able to care for him in the home he loved until the illness reached tipping point and he needed full-time nursing. After nearly four decades of a shared life I was suddenly faced with the stark reality of being on my own. No longer cooking for two it would have been so easy to rely on sandwiches and fall victim to what my mother (who had been a nurse during WW2) called 'bread and butter anaemia'. Producing, preparing and cooking for myself the way she did after my father died, has become an on-going spiritual, life-enhancing discipline and never a chore.

I have been enchanted, some might say obsessed, with gardening since 1985 when Jimmy and I moved to Sussex, the county of my birth and I have the fingernails, or rather lack of them, to show for it. Once again, under the tutelage of my mother, who remained in our old family home three miles away, I learned to propagate flowers and to grow fruit and vegetables, the plot so large it is nicknamed 'the allotment'. Accompanied down the garden by a four-footed friend, knife and colander in hand, I cannot express the pleasure of selecting what to pick or dig up in order to create a tasty meal. The added bonuses are manifold with zero air miles and every organic mouthful bursting with taste and freshness.

'Lunch was absolutely delicious and everything looked so beautiful, down to the prettiest napkins. You have to do a "Bryony" book. Your illustrations, your photos, your recipes, your flowers in divine vases, your gardening tips like the one about snipping a bit out of the courgette flowers to let the water drain off... All grist to the material. Has to be done. Your home and garden are a dream.'

PATTIE BARRON, GARDENING JOURNALIST, *LONDON EVENING STANDARD*

The whole ethos behind my style of cooking is that not one recipe is set in stone and can easily be adapted to your own individual tastes and needs or for several hungry mouths. Also, and I apologise in advance, I tend not to measure the ingredients, my gut instinct telling me it will always taste good. However, in order to help those who rely on some sort of guideline, I have tried to include quantities here and there as best I can.

My Gentleman Jim – a love story, was published in October 2015. Since then I have been itching to re-commit pen to paper and the inspiration for this book came from friends who encouraged me to collate my random jottings, simple recipes, tips and photographs taken from the kitchen window and beyond of animals, birds and flowers recorded over the last few tumultuous years.

Grow Happy, Cook Happy, Be Happy is the result. I have learned so much along the way, experimenting with my camera and with recipes, and I hope that my endeavours will inspire perhaps the less experienced to venture into the kitchen via the garden, allotment, balcony or window sill. There is nothing more rewarding than creating something which gives pleasure and satisfaction, and I know you will have as much fun as I do if you give it a go.

'I love all your daily posts, your delicious recipes, your wonderful photographs, your delightful art, your writing and the way you allow so many of us into your world. I see the girl I first met over 30 years ago who has evolved into a magnificent, marvellous woman and friend. How lucky we are to have you'

MW

'It was all absolutely delicious and not a morsel was left. Thank you, Bryony, for a truly fabulous meal. When are you opening a restaurant?'

JM

'I did your fishcakes the other night for supper. Delicious'

ED

'On every occasion that I have seen photographs of your creations I have found myself drooling with anticipation of having my taste buds stimulated with food, glorious food. I feel confident that your book will be a great success despite the plethora of books on cookery. I hope you find someone who will celebrate your unique persona'

MS

'Your photographic skills are second to none. You have an amazing garden with wonderful wildlife all beautifully captured on camera through the seasons. Who needs spring? Just need your regular bulletins'

CH

'I love your recipes for inspiration. They are perfect and so doable'

RD

Contents

SUMMER

top: *Making himself at home*
bottom: *A childhood favourite*

JUNE 1ST *I am overwhelmed with the rabbit invasion in the garden, which at times, resembles an open audition for a sequel to* Watership Down. *Getting my own back is on the cards, to quote Isaac Barrow (sermon XXXIII): 'It is commonly said that revenge is sweet, but to a calm and considerate mind, patience and forgiveness are sweeter.'*

Chocolate blancmange bunny is even nicer.

If you don't have a vintage bunny jelly mould in your cupboard, they can be picked up at boot fairs and charity shops.

Chocolate bunny blancmange

INGREDIENTS

1 standard pack of green jelly
2½ cups milk
1 heaped tbsp granulated sugar
1 tbsp cornflour
1 heaped tbsp cocoa powder
a few currants
1 can whipped cream

In advance make your jelly according to the pack instructions. To speed up setting pour into a shallow dish and put in the fridge.

Keep a little of the cold milk aside, then gently heat the rest with the sugar in a pan. Put the cornflour and cocoa into a small bowl and dilute with the reserved cold milk – never use hot milk on cornflour as it will go lumpy. Add this to the warm milk and whisk until it comes to a gentle boil. Cook for about a minute, stirring all the while, then pour into your rabbit mould and cover with clingfilm – this will prevent a skin from developing. When cool, chill in the fridge.

Run the mould quickly under a hot tap to loosen the blancmange, rinse a serving dish with a little water and place on top of the mould. Up-end and the rabbit will come free.

Chop up the green jelly 'grass' and spoon around the bunny. Squirt a little cream to make a fluffy tail, position a couple of currants for the eyes and scatter a few more over the grass to look like droppings. Little people love this and think it's great fun.

TIP

By wetting the serving plate when you turn out the blancmange, if it isn't quite central, you will be able to slide it gently into position.

JUNE 4TH

Strawberry, elderflower and ginger cordial

Just made another batch of elderflower cordial (see page 239) but with a twist: I added fresh strawberries and a piece of root ginger to the mix. It is such a pretty pink and made a lovely long drink: one large glass filled with a measure of the elderflower, strawberry and ginger cordial, plus a dash of Angostura bitters over lots of ice, topped up with fizzy water and two sprigs of mint.

TIP

Make a pot of tea, strain and allow to cool. Pour into a jug and sweeten with elderflower cordial. Add lots of ice, fresh mint and a sliced lemon.

above: *Perfect for a summer's day*

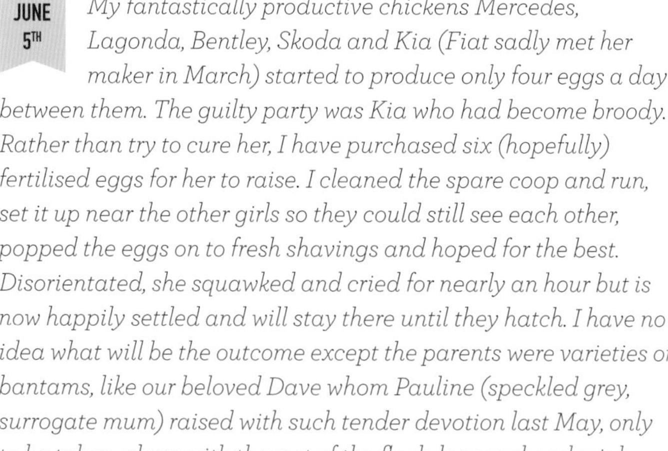

JUNE 5TH *My fantastically productive chickens Mercedes, Lagonda, Bentley, Skoda and Kia (Fiat sadly met her maker in March) started to produce only four eggs a day between them. The guilty party was Kia who had become broody. Rather than try to cure her, I have purchased six (hopefully) fertilised eggs for her to raise. I cleaned the spare coop and run, set it up near the other girls so they could still see each other, popped the eggs on to fresh shavings and hoped for the best. Disorientated, she squawked and cried for nearly an hour but is now happily settled and will stay there until they hatch. I have no idea what will be the outcome except the parents were varieties of bantams, like our beloved Dave whom Pauline (speckled grey, surrogate mum) raised with such tender devotion last May, only to be taken, along with the rest of the flock, by vagabond mink. Fingers crossed we are more successful this time around.*

above: *RIP beautiful Dave, an absolute star*
below: *Beetroot salad*

Beetroot salad

INGREDIENTS

- 1 raw beetroot, spiralised
- 6 black olives, stoned and cut into small pieces
- 4 spring onions, sliced
- 1 raw baby turnip, spiralised
- 1 small courgette, spiralised
- 1 ripe avocado, sliced
- juice of ½ lemon
- olive oil
- splash of vinegar (any type other than malt)
- salt and ground black pepper
- basil leaves and parsley, roughly chopped or torn

Mix all the ingredients bar the avocado with the dressing made from the lemon juice, olive oil, vinegar and salt and pepper. Arrange on a plate with the sliced avocado and serve at once.

JUNE 6TH *Blown down the garden and back again by 50mph gusts of wind to pick a bowl of lettuce, asparagus and garlic, which were turned into a creamy soup (with the addition of a small onion) in under 15 minutes. And the first strawberries.*

My broody girl was very distressed so I moved the coop nearer to the main run, but to no avail. I was worried that the eggs were not being kept warm and decided to return her to the others. I placed the eggs in the nesting box and released her. She went immediately up the little ladder into the coop, where she has remained since. They should be incubated for about 21 or so days apparently and I will endeavour to move her back into her own quarters a few days before the chicks are due to hatch otherwise there is a strong likelihood they will be killed by the other hens. Parenthood is so full of worries...

Well, at last we have had some decent rain. It started yesterday afternoon and fell solidly throughout the night, a welcome relief for every farmer and gardener. The strong winds have mercifully abated and the wild flower meadow is gradually changing colour from snowy, frothy white to having dots of magenta from the corn cockles. Butterflies abound.

above: *A sun-kissed treat*
below: *The wild flower meadow in all its glory*

Artichoke and asparagus vegetable bake

INGREDIENTS

4 eggs
½ tub crème fraîche
1 cup grated cheese (such as Cheddar, Emmental or Gruyère)
1 tbsp fresh chives, chopped
salt and ground black pepper
1 bunch of asparagus, cut into 2.5cm (1in) pieces
6 small roasted artichokes (from a jar) cut into rough chunks
several sunblush dried tomatoes, roughly chopped

Preheat the oven to 200°C (180°C fan) mark 6. Mix the eggs and crème fraîche together, then add the cheese and chives. Season with salt and pepper. Cover the bottom of a buttered shallow gratin dish with the asparagus, artichokes and tomatoes. Pour on the egg mixture and bake in the oven for about 30 minutes, or until it has set and the top is golden brown. Eat warm with a green salad.

above: *Artichoke flowers and lavender for the table*
right: *Ingredients for artichoke and asparagus bake*

I can eke out two or three days' worth of meals from one large chicken (not including stock made from the bones) and this was a recipe for day two.

Chicken risotto

Take a large shallow pan or deep frying pan and heat over a moderate heat. Add the butter and oil, then add the onion and sweat it for about 5 minutes, stirring all the while. Add the red pepper and cook for a further minute or two, then add the garlic and throw in the rice. Fry for about 3 minutes, add the wine then the stock, ladle by ladle. Take your time doing this – you are aiming at a soupy, creamy consistency. During the last 15–20 minutes of cooking add the asparagus, chicken and more stock if needed and season. Cover the pan, reduce the heat and continue until most of the liquid is absorbed and the rice cooked through. Stir in the parsley, lots more butter and the Parmesan. Serve in bowls.

INGREDIENTS

- a good lump of butter, plus extra to stir in at the end
- a splash of olive oil
- 1 large onion, finely sliced
- ½ red pepper, deseeded and sliced
- 1 large garlic clove, chopped
- 1½ cups Arborio rice
- 1 large glass of white wine
- 1¼ cups hot strong chicken stock
- 1 bunch of asparagus, cut into 2.5cm (1in) pieces
- leftover roast chicken picked from the carcass
- salt and ground black pepper
- 1 tbsp fresh parsley, chopped
- lots of grated Parmesan cheese

left: *Chicken risotto*

JUNE 7TH

I make porridge most mornings for breakfast but when the sun is shining and there is the promise of a fine day, and it's maybe warm enough to eat in the garden, I have started making this quick, nourishing muesli.

Oaty breakfast

INGREDIENTS

- 1 cup porridge oats
- 1 tbsp mixed pumpkin and sunflower seeds
- 1 eating apple, cut into small chunks, skin on
- 1 tbsp sultanas
- blueberries, if you like

Turn on the grill or preheat the oven to 200°C (180°C fan) mark 6. Spread the porridge oats on to a metal baking dish and toast under the grill or in the oven until they begin to take on a slight nutty brown colour – too much and they will burn. When cool, put into a bowl with the seeds, apple and sultanas and/or some blueberries if you have any. Eat straightaway with some really cold milk.

right: *The raisin thief*

JUNE 8TH *This morning I bought two (not too large) plaice from our wet fish shop in the village. James topped and tailed them but kept them on the bone plus the skin. Opposite at the greengrocer's I bought a bunch of watercress and some raw, locally grown beetroot. Once home, I twisted off the leaves and placed the beets in a pan, covering them with cold water. Once they came to the boil I reduced the heat and left them to simmer gently for about an hour until soft enough to pierce with a skewer. I drained them, refreshed them with cold water and removed the skins by slipping them off with my fingers slicing them into a bowl, keeping them warm to have with the fish.*

above: *An embarrassment of riches*

Plaice with fresh watercress sauce and beetroot

To make the watercress sauce, put the shallot into a small saucepan with the wine and allow to cook gently for 5 minutes, or until it is soft and the wine almost evaporated. Transfer the shallot to a small blender along with the watercress and other sauce ingredients and whizz until smooth. Put into a bowl and then cool in the fridge.

Rinse the fish under the cold tap and dry on kitchen paper. Heat a frying pan with a small amount of oil (adding butter for flavour once the fish is almost cooked). Lightly coat the fish with some flour and put them, white skin side down first, into the hot pan. Cook gently for 3 minutes, because you want the centre along the backbone to be cooked through, and then turn to cook the other side for a further 5 minutes, adding the butter and basting the fish as it's cooking. Season with salt and pepper and serve with the cold watercress sauce, some sliced beetroot and buttered wholemeal bread.

INGREDIENTS

FOR THE WATERCRESS SAUCE

1 small shallot, very finely chopped
about 2 tbsp dry white wine
1 small bunch (or bag) of watercress
2 tbsp crème fraîche
juice of ½ lemon
salt and ground black pepper

FOR THE PLAICE

1 plaice per person
vegetable or sunflower oil
30g (1oz) butter
plain flour to dust

above: *Summer unfurls*

INGREDIENTS

- olive oil
- 1 medium onion, finely sliced
- 6 medium tomatoes, cut into small pieces
- 1 tbsp concentrated tomato purée
- 1–2 garlic cloves, crushed or chopped
- salt and ground black pepper
- 2–3 cups dried pasta shapes, such as spirals, penne, etc.
- 1 standard bag of spinach or the leafy parts of Swiss chard leaves
- 1 small tub crème fraîche (half- or full-fat)
- 1 good cupful grated Emmental and/or Gruyère cheese, plus extra to sprinkle
- a little cold milk
- 1 cup fresh brown breadcrumbs
- olive oil, to drizzle or butter, if you prefer

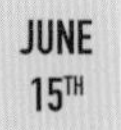

JUNE 15TH

This is a very simple pasta bake where you can actually savour the taste of the vegetables.

Quick pasta dish

Preheat the oven to 200°C (180°C fan) mark 6. Begin by making the tomato sauce. Heat a little olive oil in a saucepan over a moderate heat and add the onion. Sweat for about 5 minutes, stirring to prevent burning. Add the tomatoes, stir and cook for a further 3–4 minutes before adding the tomato purée and garlic. Add a little water, season lightly, stir, cover with a lid and simmer until the onion is soft, about 10 minutes.

In the meantime, cook the pasta in a pan of boiling salted water. Remove and drain when *al dente* (with a little bite left). Wash the spinach or Swiss chard and cook in a pan with a little water until soft. Drain well.

Put the crème fraîche into a bowl and beat with a fork before adding the grated cheese. Add a little milk until the sauce is slightly less thick. Season with salt and pepper and mix into the cooked pasta. Pour half the cheesy pasta on to the bottom of a greased gratin dish. Next, scatter the cooked spinach or chard and then pour the tomato sauce on top. Finally, add the remaining pasta.

You can prepare this in advance and then heat up in the oven for about 20 minutes until bubbling and hot through. I like a crunchy topping so before I put it into the oven I mix the breadcrumbs with some grated cheese, scatter this over the surface and then drizzle with a little olive oil, or dot with butter.

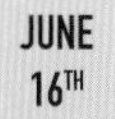

JUNE 16TH

Fennel salad

INGREDIENTS

- 1 fennel bulb, finely sliced
- 450g (1lb) fresh broad beans, podded, blanched in boiling water for 2 minutes, then popped out of their skins
- ⅓–½ cucumber, sliced
- 4–6 spring onions, sliced
- 2 tomatoes, cut into small chunks
- ⅓ pack of feta cheese, drained and crumbled
- juice of 1 lemon
- 1 medium cooked beetroot, sliced or cut into small chunks
- 1 tbsp pumpkin and sunflower seeds
- olive oil
- salt and ground black pepper
- a small handful of fresh basil leaves

TIP

How to pod broad beans: run a vegetable peeler down the 'rib' of each bean. This will open up the pod easily and speed up the process no end.

Mix everything together in a salad bowl and serve.

below: *Fresh out of the ground*

JUNE 17TH

Puy lentil salad

INGREDIENTS

1 standard pouch of cooked Puy lentils
1 celery stick, finely chopped,
4 spring onions, finely sliced
a handful of radishes, sliced
a handful of cherry tomatoes, halved
⅓ cucumber, sliced
fresh parsley, chopped
fresh basil, roughly torn

FOR THE DRESSING

1 tbsp olive oil
1 heaped tbsp natural yogurt
juice of ½ lemon
salt and ground black pepper

Mix everything together in a salad bowl, including the dressing, and serve.

above: *Cherry tomatoes*
below: *Pistachio pesto*

JUNE 18TH

I had run out of pine nuts and made a pesto with toasted pistachios.

Pistachio pesto

INGREDIENTS

1 cup pistachios
1 cup fresh basil leaves
2–3 tbsp olive oil
½ cup grated Parmesan cheese
2 garlic cloves, chopped
salt and ground black pepper

Blitz everything together in a blender or food processor and serve with pasta. If there is any left over, put into a clean jar, cover with a little more olive oil and seal with the lid. This will keep in the fridge for a week or so.

JUNE 20TH *Last night's supper with Mel in the garden was a treat. I have to say, that the salmon I cooked was the nicest I have ever tasted - and that includes the luxury in the past of wild salmon. Knowing how I love fish, salmon in particular, this recipe was given to me by a friend. She couldn't remember where it came from but I pass on my thanks to whoever had the imagination to put all these ingredients together on one dish.*

Measurements are according to how much fish you are cooking.

above: *Marinated salmon steaks with peas, broad beans and chorizo*

Marinated salmon steaks with peas, broad beans and chorizo

INGREDIENTS

- 1 salmon steak per person
- finely grated zest and juice of 1 lemon
- olive oil
- 1 tsp smoked paprika or Pimentón
- a few fresh thyme sprigs, leaves picked off
- salt and ground black pepper
- fresh peas
- fresh broad beans
- best-quality chorizo
- 1 lemon
- a handful of fresh mint, chopped
- a handful of radishes, sliced
- a few asparagus spears, cooked and cut into 2.5cm (1 in) pieces

Marinate the salmon steaks in the lemon juice and zest, a little olive oil, smoked paprika, thyme leaves and salt and pepper for 30 minutes –1 hour.

Light your barbecue. Cook the peas and broad beans, separately, in a little boiling water for 2–3 minutes. When the latter are done, refresh under cold water and remove the skins. Add to the peas and keep at room temperature. Peel off the skin from some chorizo and cut into small pieces, then fry in a small frying pan for 3–4 minutes until crisp. Drain and add the chorizo oil to the peas and beans.

Place the salmon, skin side up, on the barbecue and cook for 1–2 minutes. Cut the lemon in half and place next to the fish, cut side down. Turn the fish over and finish cooking for a further 5 or so minutes.

Mix the mint with the radishes and asparagus and add to the peas and broad beans followed by the crispy chorizo, plus a little more olive oil. I served this with Jersey Royal potatoes steamed over more mint.

Panacotta with strawberries

INGREDIENTS

3 leaves gelatine
250ml (9fl oz) full fat milk
250ml (9fl oz) double cream
2 tsp caster sugar
1 tsp vanilla extract
a handful of strawberries, cut in half
juice from 2 passion fruit, sieved to remove the pips

Soak the gelatine according to the pack instructions. Warm the milk, cream, sugar and vanilla in a pan, then add the softened gelatine, stirring until it has dissolved. Pour the mixture into a pretty jelly mould and allow it to set in the fridge until soft. Serve with the strawberries soaked in the passion fruit juice.

As an alternative I made a small amount of jelly using Prosecco and some elderflower cordial. I let this set in a pretty dish before making a panacotta with some white chocolate. Decorated with strawberries, raspberries and blueberries it made a wonderful, albeit, rather rich pudding.

above: *Sweet and delicious*
right: *Prosecco panacotta*

JUNE 21ST *They say that hot food on a hot day is a good way of coping with the heat so I have made the following soup to test the theory. It is an excellent way of using lettuces, which are beginning to bolt (run to seed).*

Lettuce soup

INGREDIENTS

1 large leek, finely sliced
1 large celery stick, sliced
1 large carrot, finely chopped
olive oil
2½ cups chicken stock
2 little gem lettuces, sliced
salt and ground black pepper
1 cup full fat milk

In a saucepan, sweat the leek, celery and carrot in a little oil for 2 minutes over a moderate heat, then add the chicken stock. Bring to the boil, reduce the heat and simmer for about 10 minutes. Add the lettuces, stir and cook for a further 2 minutes. Blitz in a liquidiser or use a hand-held blender, season with salt and pepper and add the milk. It is a really refreshing soup: light, delicate and delicious.

above: *Trouble on the hop*
left: *Lettuce soup*

JUNE 24TH

Prawn salad

INGREDIENTS

1 Chinese radish, grated, or a bunch of ordinary radishes, sliced
1 small turnip, grated
450g (1lb) fresh broad beans or frozen, cooked briefly and their skins removed
1 little gem lettuce, leaves torn
1 small green pepper, deseeded and finely chopped or sliced
1 small bunch of asparagus, cut into 2.5cm (1in) pieces and lightly steamed
1 standard pack of ready-cooked cold water North Atlantic prawns
1 tbsp olive oil
2 tsp cider or white wine vinegar
juice of ½ lemon
salt and ground black pepper
1 heaped tbsp good-quality mayonnaise (optional)

Mix everything together in a salad bowl and serve with the mayonnaise (if included) and lemon slices in a separate bowl.

above: *Baby turnips*
right: *Prawn salad*

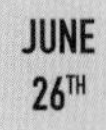

JUNE 26TH

Another easy-to-prepare in advance summer lunch.

Salmon with watercress sauce

INGREDIENTS

1 salmon fillet per person
lemon slices
sliced fennel
1 garlic clove, sliced
2 bay leaves
white wine, if you like
salt and ground black pepper
lemon wedges to garnish

FOR THE SAUCE:

1 bunch or bag of watercress, roughly chopped
4 spring onions, roughly chopped
½ tub crème fraîche
1 tbsp good-quality mayonnaise
salt and pepper

Preheat the oven to 200°C (180°C fan) mark 6. Begin by tearing off a large piece of baking parchment and laying it on a baking tray. Place the salmon on top along with a couple of slices of lemon per fillet, a few slices of fennel, the garlic, bay leaves and a dash of white wine, if using. Season well and carefully fold the parchment, pleating the seams to make a parcel. Bake in the oven for about 8–10 minutes maximum. Allow to cool in the parchment.

To make the sauce, put the watercress and spring onion into a blender along with the crème fraîche and mayonnaise and blitz, but not too much. Check for seasoning and put into a pretty bowl.

Unwrap the salmon and gently lift off the skin before putting on to individual plates or a small serving dish. Garnish with lemon wedges and serve with the sauce, steamed new potatoes and a salad of your choice.

top: *Beautiful bay leaves on tap*
bottom: *Pink magnolia and green grasshopper*

JUNE 30TH *A fitting end to a wonderful month: lunch in the garden with youngest nephew Tom and his fiancée Faith Ann who are over from Los Angeles where they live and work. They are getting married this Saturday and have asked me to do the flowers for her bouquet so, after lunch we shall wander around the garden so she can choose what to put in it. Their wedding will take place at my brother Paul's farm in Kent under the weeping willow in the meadow by the lake. It will be magical.*

above: *Faith-Ann's meadow bouquet*

Rainbow raw root salad

INGREDIENTS

1 beetroot, peeled and grated
1 carrot, peeled and grated
1 fennel bulb, finely sliced
a handful of rocket leaves
1 baby turnip, peeled and grated
1 red onion, finely chopped
1 tbsp pumpkin and sunflower seeds
1 celery stick, finely sliced
1 small green pepper, deseeded and finely sliced
1 tbsp olive oil
2 tsp cider vinegar
juice of ½ lemon
salt and ground black pepper
choice of fresh herbs, such as parsley, chives, mint and basil, chopped

Mix everything together in a salad bowl and serve.

right: *Is there a crock of gold?*

Simple tuna salad

INGREDIENTS

- a few asparagus spears
- 1 small can tuna in brine or oil per person, drained
- several leftover cooked new potatoes, if available or freshly cooked and cooled, cut in half or smallish pieces, not sliced
- 1 small fennel bulb, finely sliced
- handful cherry tomatoes, quartered
- 1 beetroot, cooked, peeled and cut into small chunks
- 1 bunch of spring onions, trimmed and washed
- juice of ½ lemon, slice the remaining half for a garnish
- 450g (1lb) fresh raw baby broad beans (weight in pods)
- salt and ground black pepper
- 1 little gem lettuce per person, separated out into leaves
- 1 heaped tbsp good-quality mayonnaise
- 1 hard-boiled egg per person

Lightly steam the asparagus and refresh under the cold tap. Cut into fine slices on the diagonal and mix with the tuna, potatoes, fennel, tomatoes, beetroot, spring onions, lemon juice and beans. Season lightly and lay on top of the lettuce leaves. Spoon on the mayonnaise and garnish with lemon slices and sliced egg.

above: *Perfect for a summer lunch*

below: *So much to choose from*

The weather is glorious so here are a few refreshing beverages.

Cheapskate's 'Pimm's'

INGREDIENTS

Angostura bitters
gin
dry ginger ale
lemonade
strawberries or summer fruit of your choice
cucumber slices
mint sprigs

Take a glass (or jug) and ¾ fill it with ice cubes. Drop in a few splashes of Angostura bitters followed by a good slug of gin. Add equal measures of dry ginger ale and lemonade, stir and add fruit of your choice, cucumber and sprigs of mint.

I read that when John Major was ensconced at 10 Downing Street his caterer mixed Pimm's with tonic water, which is less sweet than lemonade and more refreshing. On the other hand, you could try this intriguing recipe for the Andrew Fuse cocktail, opposite, (copied verbatim) given to my great-great grandmother Emily Campbell in India in the early 1900s. Try it at your peril.

above: *Home is where the heart is*
below: *Archway to my corner of heaven*

This drink is one of great-great granny Emily's recipes –perfect for a summer's day.

Ice cube coffee

'Make coffee as usual only double the strength – use 2 heaping [sic] tablespoons of coffee to each cup [300ml/½ pint] of water. Pour the freshly made coffee into an ice-cube tray and freeze. A tray of these coffee cubes can be kept for instant use. Now when iced coffee is wanted, simply heat milk. Do not bring milk to the boil and do not use cream. Fill a glass with the frozen coffee cubes. Then fill with warm milk – instantly you have a delicious, refreshing iced coffee of consistency similar to iced coffee served with expensive cream.'

Andrew Fuse (in his own words)

This drink sounds vicious (and is) but it tastes very (harmful) [this was crossed out] *harmless. I once gave a teetotal maiden aunt four in quick succession telling her they were soft drinks.* Note *She cut me out of her will.*

Glass: Champaigne [sic] glass smeared with lemon and dusted with sugar.

Base: Equal parts: Benedictine, rye whisky, brandy, square gin. This should be mixed in iced shaker.

Topping: Suggest chilled dry ginger ale with coiled lemon and orange peel.

above: *High summer*

Andrew Fuse.

Glass: Champaigne glass smeared with lemon & dusted with sugar.

Base: Equal parts: Benedictine
Rye whisky
Brandy
Square Gin.

This should be mixed in iced shaker.

Topping Suggest chilled dry ginger ale with coiled lemon & orange peel.

Note. This drink sounds vicious (and is) but it tastes very ~~harmful~~. harmless. I once gave a teetotal maiden aunt four in quick sucsession telling her they were soft drinks. NB. She cut me out of her will.

The salad I had in the Friends' dining room at the Royal Academy Summer Exhibition was so fresh I am endeavouring to recreate it for lunch today.

Delicate summer salad

INGREDIENTS

- 1 cup petits pois (frozen)
- 1 cup baby broad beans (fresh or frozen)
- 1 cup pea shoots
- a handful of rocket leaves
- 4cm (1½in) slice of feta cheese, crumbled
- 1 heaped tbsp natural yogurt
- juice of ½–1 lemon
- salt and ground black pepper
- fresh, chopped herbs, such as parsley, basil, chives or dill

OPTIONAL EXTRAS

- hard-boiled egg, sliced or chopped
- radishes, sliced or chopped

Lightly blanch the peas and baby broad beans, and when cool, mix with the pea shoots, rocket and crumbled feta cheese. Toss in the dressing made from the yogurt, lemon juice, salt, pepper and fresh herbs. Add egg and radishes if you like.

TIP

Pea shoots are so easy to grow yourself, even if you don't have a garden.

above: *Delicate summer salad*
below: *Pea shoots and cut-and-come-again delights*

Growing fruit and vegetables is hard work and often soul-destroying when your efforts are snookered from lack of rain or too many frosty nights and attacks from rabbits, slugs and snails. However, when it all comes together there can be fewer more generous and rewarding pastimes. Today, I picked red- and blackcurrants, and not wishing to waste a single berry, turned them into jelly, the strawberries into jam and a mixture of tayberries and raspberries gently stewed for pudding.

The blackcurrant bushes are groaning with fruit but if I don't hurry, the birds will beat me to it. The easiest way to harvest is follows: on a dry day, cut away the whole branches bearing currants and lay them on a cloth on the ground under a tree, or on a table, then remove the fruit by gently raking your fingers along the stalks. By doing this you are also pruning away the old wood: two jobs done in one.

Jewel salad

Mix the yogurt and mayonnaise together; you may need to 'slacken' it with a little water. Pour it over the other ingredients in a salad bowl, mix well and serve. Like most of my salads (unless they contain lettuce), if it's not finished, it will keep until the following day.

INGREDIENTS

1 tbsp natural yogurt
1 tbsp good-quality mayonnaise
1 courgette, spiralised or cut very thinly into strips with a vegetable peeler
1 bunch of crispy radishes, sliced
1 bunch of watercress
fresh mint leaves, to taste
fresh parsley, to taste
fresh basil leaves, to taste
1 tub of small mozzarella balls or pearls
1 tbsp sunflower hearts
1 tbsp pumpkin seeds

above: *Home grown goodies*
left: *Jewel salad*

Sweet potato and chilli soup

INGREDIENTS

- 1 sweet potato, peeled and cut into small chunks
- 1 red chilli (deseeded if less heat required), roughly chopped
- 1 celery stick, roughly chopped
- 1 red onion, roughly chopped
- 2½ cups chicken stock
- 1 standard bag or 1 bunch of watercress
- 1 cup milk
- salt and ground black pepper

Put the potato, chilli, celery and onion into a pan with the stock and cook for about 10 minutes. For flavour, I always make mine using the leftover carcass and bits from a roasted fowl, but a stock cube or stock pot are fine. Add the watercress 5 minutes before the end. Blitz with a hand-held blender, then pour in the milk, whizz again and season to taste. Virtually zero fat and so good for the system.

above: *Simple soup ingredients*
right: *Colours of the rainbow*

Last night we had pasta shells and, as usual, I overestimated and cooked too much. Rather than give it to the chickens or Charlie (our much-loved yellow Labrador with tiny legs) I made this salad.

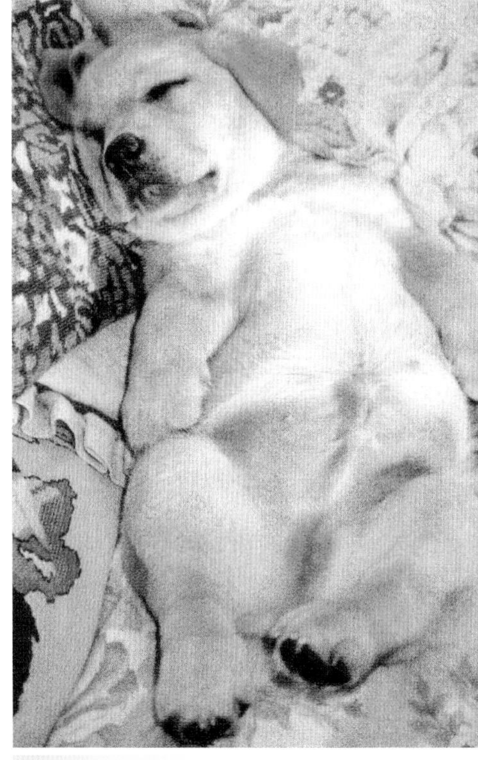

Prawn and pasta salad

INGREDIENTS

- 2–3 tbsp crème fraîche or natural yogurt
- 2–3 tbsp good-quality mayonnaise
- about 1 measuring jug or two (cold) cooked pasta shapes
- 1 standard pack of ready-cooked cold water North Atlantic prawns
- 1 small bunch of spring onions, finely sliced
- 2 cups baby broad beans and/or petits pois (frozen are fine; cooked for 3 minutes in boiling salted water. Cool quickly, then remove the outer skins of the beans if used)
- fresh herbs, such as chives, parsley
- grated zest and juice of ½ lemon
- salt and ground black pepper
- a dash or two or three of Tabasco sauce
- 1 celery stick and 7.5cm (3in) piece cucumber, sliced, also make good additions
- paprika, to sprinkle
- 1 tub of cress

Mix the crème fraîche or yogurt with the mayo, then stir in all the other ingredients except the paprika and cress. Sprinkle the top with paprika and the cress to make it pretty. Serve chilled.

top: *Our little chap*
bottom: *A paradise for wildlife*

JULY 8TH

In one corner of the garden we have a cherry plum tree. Countless others are also to be found growing wild in the hedgerows along the field boundaries where I walk Suzie (my black rescue Labrador I adopted after Charlie). The delicate white blossom in spring results in hundreds of small golden, purple or red fruits, which can be stewed or made into jam and chutney. It was a hot day and as fortune would have it, I was wearing a hat – the perfect receptacle.

We are nearing the end of the tayberry harvest and I still have hundreds of gooseberries to pick, which I keep on putting off because of the viciously sharp thorns. When I finally got around to it I combined them with the remaining tayberries and made several pounds of jelly. It went extremely well with both lamb and chicken and made a pleasant change from the traditional redcurrant.

Here is the recipe for the best strawberry jam ever.

Strawberry jam

INGREDIENTS

strawberries (for quantity see method)
jam sugar with added pectin (for quantity see method)
1 large lemon
butter

TIP

I make apricot jam in the same way.

Weigh your untrimmed fruit – you will need about 675g (1½lb). Rinse them under the tap, then remove the hulls with a knife. Place in a large bowl. Measure the equivalent weight of jam sugar and add to the strawberries, plus the juice of the lemon, and stir. Cover with a cloth and allow to macerate for as long as you can – even overnight.

After a few hours, the sugar will have dissolved and the strawberries will be soaking in the most heavenly scented syrup. Pour into a preserving (or large) pan and heat gently, stirring every now and again to prevent burning, breaking up the fruit with a potato masher. When the jam comes to the boil, stir in a knob of butter – this will help prevent too much scum from forming, which must be scooped off. The jam needs to reach a temperature of 225°C (440°F), but if you don't have a jam thermometer, don't worry – when it becomes thickish do the wrinkle test (see page 5).

Using a funnel, carefully pour the jam into hot sterilised jars (see page 5), seal immediately and store in a cool place for up to six months.

Earlier this afternoon I heard squawks coming from the garden and saw a red kite, recognisable from its distinctive 'v'-shaped tail feathers flying over next door's field where the hay was being cut. Then two buzzards appeared from nowhere resulting in a dogfight. Crows, who were responsible for the alarm calls, gathered in a huddle on the neighbouring trees; safety in numbers.

The new wild flower meadow and pond is a secret place hidden by grasses, knapweed, wild carrot, viper's bugloss, scabious and ox-eye daisies and has become the perfect spot to sit in the evening light and reflect on the day.

above, left to right: *Buzzard with its prey, aerial acrobatics, safety in numbers*
below: *The wildlife pond and here be dragonflies*

top: *A perfect omelette*
bottom: *Thank you, girls*

JULY 10TH *Today, the girls presented me with three lovely eggs, which was enough to make an omelette for the two of us the way I was taught by a Parisian taxi driver in the 1970s; the only difference being I jazzed it up with some leftover vegetables.*

Plain omelette

INGREDIENTS
1–2 eggs per person
salt and ground black pepper
a large knob of soft butter, plus extra to fry
a dash of milk

Beat the eggs in a bowl with some salt and pepper, then add the soft butter and a dash of milk.

Drop a little extra butter, about the size of a walnut, into a hot non-stick pan, swirling it around as it melts and then – only then – when it stops sizzling and begins to turn a light nutty brown, in go the eggs.

Swizzle the eggs with the flat side of a fork scraping the mixture to the centre of the pan until the base is firm but the top is a tiny bit runny (it will carry on cooking). Fold the omelette in two and serve immediately. However, I added the vegetables (leftover from yesterday), spreading them roughly over the omelette before putting it under a hot grill for a couple of minutes to finish cooking and puff up.

Well, after 30 years when Edwina Currie put the kibosh on eating runny or raw eggs, particularly for the old and very young, it is now officially safe for everyone to enjoy nature's little miracles as they wish. There seems to be a great deal of palaver over the cooking of something so simple as boiled and poached eggs, but if you follow my instructions you will not fail to please your nearest and dearest should they order one for their breakfast.

The great rule of thumb is that the fresher they are the firmer the raw albumen (the white) will be, but on the other hand, a very fresh egg will take slightly longer to cook when boiled.

The perfect poached egg

Have ready a pan of boiling water - a bit deeper than a milk pan - to which you add ½ tsp white vinegar. Don't use red wine or malt vinegar as it will colour the cooked white. Crack the egg into a small dish, check for pieces of shell and drop into the boiling water.

There is absolutely no need to whisk, stir or whizz the water first. Allow the egg to cook for a couple of minutes or more if you want it slightly firmer then, using a slotted spoon, carefully lift it out of the pan on to a piece of kitchen paper to drain. Have ready your buttered toast, season lightly with salt and pepper and enjoy. To add extra energy and oomph, eat with either some wilted baby spinach or grilled tomatoes, which give you all sorts of extra goodness when cooked.

TIP

If there is any shell, remove it by using one empty half of shell, which will attract the errant intruder like a magnet.

The perfect boiled egg

Once again, the fresher the better. Place the egg in a pan and cover with cold water. Bring it gently to the boil and cook for a couple of minutes. Then, using a spoon, lift out the egg and study how quickly the water evaporates from the shell: the quicker the egg dries, the hotter the inside of the egg, the more it is cooked. If the water is slow to disappear, replace it in the boiling water for a further 30 seconds or so. This is virtually fail proof and was the way Jimmy taught me.

left: *Egg and soldiers*

JULY 11TH

I woke to the dawn chorus at 4.30 this morning and groaned when I saw yet more rain had fallen during the night. However, the sun has come out giving the promise of a dry, warmer and less windy day. The change in temperature has unsettled the bees and a swarm gathered overnight on the low branches of the young pink variegated maple we planted in memory of Ma. I rang the Paynes brothers who already have positioned eight of their hives in our meadow. They will come later on today to collect them and find them a new home – maybe here.

For the last two weeks, I have been up to my eyes in yet more soft fruit. It is a busy time. This is my great-great grandmother Emily's recipe for gooseberry chutney.

Gooseberry chutney

INGREDIENTS

675g (1½lb) gooseberries
115g (4oz) raisins
1 level tbsp salt
1 tsp mustard seeds
175g (6oz) brown sugar, such as demerara or soft light brown sugar (the choice is yours)
2 onions, finely chopped
55g (2oz) sultanas
1 tsp ground ginger
a pinch of cayenne pepper (more if you prefer more heat)
a good pinch (¼ tsp) of ground turmeric

Put all the ingredients into a preserving pan and bring slowly to the boil. Reduce the heat and simmer for about 1 hour, or until it has thickened, or when you draw a wooden spoon across the bottom of the pan and the mixture divides. Pour the mixture carefully into four warmed sterilised jars (see page 5) and seal. This can be eaten straight away but stores well.

NOTE

This recipe does not include vinegar.

top: *A fine day ahead*
bottom: *Possible new tenants?*

JULY 12TH *What a glorious day, which I spent in the garden with two girlfriends, all three of us widow women of strong men. There was a lot to talk about accompanied by a few tears cheek by jowl with a great deal of laughter. We considered ourselves to be very lucky.*

Jumbo prawns with Singapore noodles

After removing the heads, tails, shells and the black intestinal veins running along the backs of the raw prawns marinate them in the garlic, chilli, ginger, lemon juice, soy sauce and a dash of oil for at least 30 minutes. Cook the prawns quickly on a hot griddle pan and set aside.

Heat a wok over a high heat, add a splash of oil, tip in the Singapore noodles and the spring onions and stir-fry for 2–3 minutes. Tip in the cooked prawns and the coriander and cook for a further minute. I served it with a naked side salad of spiralised cucumber and spiralised long, pink Chinese radishes.

INGREDIENTS

- 1 standard pack of fresh raw king prawns
- 2 garlic cloves crushed (no need to peel)
- 1 red chilli, finely chopped (with or without seeds)
- 2.5cm (1in) piece fresh root ginger, peeled and grated
- juice of 1 lemon
- 3 shakes of soy sauce
- a dash of vegetable oil, plus extra to cook
- 1 pack of fresh ready-to-cook Singapore noodles
- 1 bunch of spring onions, sliced
- 1 bunch of fresh coriander, roughly chopped, stalks and all
- 1 cucumber
- 1 Chinese radish or several sliced ordinary radishes

above: *The naked salad*
left: *The cooked dish*

Homemade hummus salad plate

INGREDIENTS

- 400g (14oz) can chickpeas, rinsed thoroughly and drained
- 1–2 garlic cloves, peeled
- 1 tbsp tahini
- juice of 1 lemon
- 2 tbsp olive oil, plus extra to drizzle
- salt and ground black pepper
- smoked paprika to sprinkle

Put the chickpeas, garlic, tahini, lemon juice and olive oil into a mini blender and blitz until smooth. Taste and season accordingly. You might need to slacken it with a little cold water. Transfer the hummus to a serving dish, then drizzle a little more olive oil and dust some paprika through a fine sieve. Serve with a simple salad, such as the one in the picture of radishes, lettuce and beetroot and some warmed pitta bread.

above: *Chicken, not chickpea*
right: *Homemade hummus salad plate*

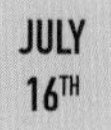

JULY 16TH

Yesterday I made this supper dish using two smallish pieces of salmon. It could easily have stretched to four people.

Salmon 'turtle' en croute

As a precaution I always give bagged veg a quick wash even if the pack says there is no need. Put the spinach in a pan with no water and cook until it wilts. Remove from the heat, run under the cold tap and strain, squeezing out as much moisture as you can.

Preheat the oven to 200°C (180°C fan) mark 6. Line a baking sheet with baking parchment. Allow the pastry to reach room temperature and roll out fairly thinly on a lightly floured surface. Roughly spread a little (about a third) of the Boursin on to the pastry then spread some of the cold spinach on top.

Rinse, pat the salmon dry and place on top of the spinach. Spread one more layer of Boursin on top. Grate the zest of the lemon over the top. Season lightly with salt (the cheese will have plenty) but give some good grindings of pepper.

Lightly beat the egg in a bowl with a dash of cold water to loosen it and brush over the outer edges of the pastry. Pull the empty side over and seal (mine turned out a rather lumpy bundle resembling a turtle, hence the name of the dish). Lift it carefully onto the prepared baking sheet. Using scissors, nick the body here and there to look like scales. I used some of the leftover pastry to shape a head and legs attaching them to the body. Brush liberally all over with more eggwash and place in the oven for about 20 minutes, or until the pastry is golden and cooked.

INGREDIENTS

- 1 standard bag of ready-washed baby spinach leaves
- ½ pack of all-butter puff pastry
- 1 Boursin cheese *aux fines herbes*
- 1 good-sized piece salmon, or a pack of 2 fillets
- ½ lemon
- salt and ground black pepper
- 1 egg

NOTE

To remove the skin from the raw fish peel a bit back with your fingers and lay it skin side down on a board. Hold on to the flap of skin and run a very sharp knife firmly against the board, between the skin and the fish.

left: *Not quite salmon-shaped*

above: *Time for tea*

JULY 17TH *After a wonderful fortnight eating more meals on the terrace than we have over the last two years, the windy weather came as a bit of a shock. It has unfortunately done quite a lot of damage, notably knocking over the sweetcorn and bashing the courgettes into oblivion, but it did bring with it some much needed rain. To celebrate the return of a sunny weekend, I made a batch of cupcakes although they are nothing like the mountainous creations, which seem to be popular at the moment. This recipe couldn't be easier.*

Old-fashioned cupcakes

INGREDIENTS

1 egg and equal weight of:
soft butter
caster sugar
self-raising flour
½ tsp baking powder
a small pinch of salt
juice and a little grated zest of either 1 lemon or an orange, a little vanilla extract or 1 heaped tsp cocoa powder per egg, if you like

TO DECORATE

icing sugar (see method right)
lemon or orange juice, water or food colouring, if you like
sprinkles

Preheat the oven to 200°C (180°C fan) mark 6. Put the egg, butter, sugar and flour into a bowl or small blender (if you use a large mixer the ingredients will get lost and won't blend). Add the baking powder, salt and an optional flavouring and whizz quickly or beat by hand for a brief moment. It will all come together within seconds.

Put some paper cases onto a tray and two-thirds fill with the cake mix. Bake on the middle shelf of the oven for about 7–8 minutes, but check after 6, by dipping a clean skewer or a very pointed knife into a cake. If the tip comes out clean, the cakes are done. If not, put them back for a minute or so more. Take out of the oven and cover with a clean cloth until they are cold enough to decorate.

For the topping, sift some icing sugar into a bowl. You will probably end up with half a dozen cakes, so 2 cups of icing sugar should be plenty. Moisten it with either the juice of the remaining lemon or orange, or water and food colouring. Go gently with the latter or it will end up the colour of Brighton rock. Spread the mixture over each cake and decorate with sprinkles. Perfect for Sunday tea under the apple tree.

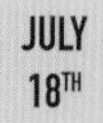

JULY 18TH

Green pepper soup

INGREDIENTS

1–2 green peppers, deseeded and roughly chopped
1–2 carrots, roughly chopped
1 red or ordinary onion, sliced
1 tbsp olive oil
2½ cups chicken or vegetable stock
a handful of fresh coriander
a little full-fat milk

The green peppers are growing fast in the greenhouse, so I picked two large enough to make into soup. Using only a few ingredients I sweated the peppers with the carrots and onion in a little olive oil over a high heat for 2–3 minutes, stirring constantly, then added the chicken stock. When the vegetables were soft I threw in the coriander, stalks and all, and blitzed it with some milk. I reckon it would make a good soup if well chilled, with a drizzle of cream and a few chives or parsley leaves sprinkled on top.

above: *Suzie in the corn fields*
below: *Coriander seedlings*
left: *Green pepper soup*

A dish cooked in the frying pan.

Courgette and chickpea savoury

INGREDIENTS

1 medium courgette, grated
1 red or green chilli, deseeded if you don't want too much heat, and finely chopped
1 red onion, finely chopped
400g (14oz) can chickpeas, rinsed, drained and slightly crushed with a potato masher
Panko breadcrumbs or fresh brown breadcrumbs
1 egg
1 tbsp grated Parmesan cheese
fresh coriander, roughly chopped
salt and ground black pepper
1 tbsp olive oil

Put the raw grated courgette into a clean napkin and squeeze out as much water as you can. Put into a bowl and add the chilli, onion, chickpeas, breadcrumbs, egg, cheese, coriander and seasoning, mixing well.

Heat the olive oil in a frying pan over a moderate heat, add the mixture and cook for about 5–6 minutes until golden brown. Turn out on to a large plate before sliding it in the pan to cook the other side. Serve warm or at room temperature.

NOTE

The chickpeas added another dimension making the texture quite crumbly. If you prefer a firmer result, add an extra egg and a tablespoon of flour.

JULY 19TH

The vegetables are growing like billy-o and, the crop exhausted, I hoicked out the broad beans and before putting the plants on to the compost heap, I rubbed off the little white bobbly nodules from the roots – these contain nitrogen and will nourish the soil for a leafy follow-on sowing. Courgettes and squashes are very thirsty and, because they tend to spread (some more than others) it is not always easy to locate where the roots are, so making watering haphazard. The problem is solved by placing a tall cane adjacent to the young courgette at the time of planting thus enabling me to direct the hose or watering can to the right spot. Regular watering and feeding is essential and, if not properly cared for, they can develop a condition called powdery mildew. This isn't the end of the world: simply cut away the damaged leaves (but do not put on the compost heap – burn them), give it some tomato food and it should pick up again.

Based on a system traditionally used by native Americans known as the 'Three Sisters' method of planting I sowed sweetcorn and pumpkin seeds around a wigwam of surplus runner bean seedlings I couldn't bear to throw away. This creates a natural symbiosis between the plants promoting healthy growth, with the leaves of the courgettes and pumpkins smothering the ground and preventing weeds from taking over.

The bed is ring-fenced by self-seeded borage whose iridescent blue flowers the bees love, their presence helping with pollination and a good crop. The courgette flowers are perfect cups for holding water and the tip of the courgette can rot before it is fully ripe. To prevent this, pierce the flower head near the base with your finger and it will drain away.

Only three of the cucumber seeds have germinated and rather than put them out in the open I planted them in the empty cold frame into which I added a bag of organic vegetable compost. With sturdy canes for them to climb up they are sheltered from strong winds, and already I have picked several decent fruits. The herb walk leading to the chickens smells wonderful as you brush past the lavender, curry plant and rosemary.

above: *The herb walk*

JULY 21ST

This is what I gathered this morning: 1 egg (lazy girls), broad beans, parsley, courgette, red onion and some beetroot. One was a bit too large so I thought I would make some soup using up stuff in the fridge.

Beetroot soup

INGREDIENTS

30g (1oz) butter
1 large onion, chopped
1 carrot, chopped
1 garlic clove, chopped
1 large stick of celery stick, chopped
450g (1lb) uncooked beetroot, peeled and grated
5 cups chicken stock (either fresh or made from a cube/granules)
salt and ground black pepper
¼ tsp dried chilli flakes
fresh parsley, chopped
cream, if you like

Melt the butter in a saucepan over a moderate heat, tip in all the vegetables, except the beetroot, stir and let them sweat for 5 minutes. Add the beetroot, stir, then add the stock, salt and pepper to taste and chilli flakes. Bring to the boil, reduce the heat and simmer until the vegetables are nice and soft. Blitz with a hand-held blender, then sprinkle with finely chopped parsley and maybe a swirl of cream and serve hot. I am not a huge fan of cold soups but I reckon that if this passed through a sieve to make it velvety, it would a refreshing change on a hot day although it might be a little too thick so add a little water or cold milk.

right: *Beetroot soup*

Today is Jimmy's birthday. I found this horoscope in one of my mother's old Good Housekeeping *magazines dated July 1951. It could have been written for him:*

'A Leo is lordly but lovable, intensely faithful, honourable. A born leader; ambitious, romantic, sociable, benevolent; idealistic, conventional, self-assured. A good organiser, creative. He demands the limelight. No use trying to keep him all to yourself, for he is essentially a gregarious person. You will always take first place in his heart.'

This 'picky-picky' lunch is typical of the sort of meal I love to prepare with whatever is available, time permitting, one of the stars being braised baby artichokes *(see page 243)**.*

above: *Jimmy sharing his sandwich*
below: *Picky-picky lunch*

Picky-picky lunch

INGREDIENTS
1 pack of smoked trout fillets
bowl of lettuce with a light vinaigrette dressing made from sunflower oil
tomato, cucumber and onion salad
crusty loaf

REMOULADE INGREDIENTS
1 celeriac root
2 tbs good-quality mayonnaise
1 heaped tsp Dijon mustard
chopped parsley

Remove the outer skin of the celeriac with a vegetable knife and any craggy, muddy bits. Cut it into manageable chunks and grate them into a bowl. In a separate dish, stir the mayonnaise with the Dijon mustard and adjust seasoning - a few twists of freshly ground pepper is probably all you need. Add this to the grated celeriac and mix well. I believe you eat first with your eyes and therefore presentation is paramount: put the remoulade into a pretty dish, sprinkling it with some chopped parsley. Serve with the trout, lettuce, salad and bread. Remoulade also goes particularly well with Parma ham.

TIP
Other additions to the meal, depending on what I have available might include cooked beetroot, salad leaves, asparagus, hardboiled eggs, or other cold meats.

JULY 23RD

The garden resonates with the sound of constant cheeping.

I took these pictures during the space of an hour at the kitchen window – much more fun than doing the ironing. From outside my bedroom window this morning came a chirrup I didn't recognise – a baby wren. The new bird feeder is a hive of activity and yesterday I watched a family of recently fledged goldfinches pestering their parents to be fed, their wings whirring and fluttering to grab attention.

On Thursday afternoon Charlie started barking furiously. It was the low loader arriving with the ancient remains of the chassis of a shepherd's hut and the beginning of a dream I have long harboured. It will be a wonderful bolt hole, a sanctuary, a place to sit and think in peace and quiet. My older brother Paul meditates every day and asked me which direction I am going to have it pointing towards, I replied, overlooking the water meadow. 'Perfect, that couldn't be better. Just make sure you line it up to the magnetic East.'

After very full-on eating at the weekend a light supper beckoned if only to prevent night starvation.

above: *Baby robin*
bottom: *My dream has begun*

Mixed vegetable stir-fry

INGREDIENTS

1 tbsp sunflower oil
1 baby yellow courgette
1 baby green courgette
15cm (6in) piece cucumber, cut into tiny strips
a few chard leaves, roughly chopped
1 garlic clove, chopped
1 purple sprouting broccoli sprig
¼ sweetheart cabbage, finely sliced
2.5cm (1in) piece fresh root ginger, peeled and grated
soy sauce
1 nest of rice noodles per person, cooked according to pack instructions

I heated the wok over a high heat, added the oil and threw in all the vegetables and ginger, stirring quickly before covering with a lid so that they could cook in the steam for a couple of minutes. Then I added a good tablespoon of soy, stirred again, then the noodles. These will need reheating for a further minute or so.

above: *Purple sprouting broccoli*
right: *Another noodle and vegetable stir-fry*

JULY 24TH *I want to share with you this recipe given to me by a friend Mr P, but I have to confess that until last night I hadn't actually cooked it. It made a pleasant change from plain old bangers and onion gravy. When I was having a little scratch among the weeds in the large border yesterday in all that humid heat, I found a flourishing rogue potato plant. The original tuber must have been in the compost laid on the beds in the spring and, on lifting it, there was over a pound of beautiful red spuds.*

Mr P's sausage special

INGREDIENTS

- 1 white or red onion or shallot, finely chopped
- 1 celery stick, chopped
- the best outdoor reared pork sausages
- potatoes, cut into wedges
- 1 white or red onion/shallot
- olive oil to drizzle
- salt and ground black pepper
- 2 fresh rosemary sprigs, chopped
- 2 fresh thyme sprigs, chopped
- 2 or more eating apples depending on size (I used Pink Lady), cored

Preheat the oven to 200°C (180°C fan) mark 6. Spread the onion out in a shallow baking dish, then add the celery. Separate the sausages but don't prick them and place on top of the onion and celery. Add the potatoes to the dish. Drizzle a little olive oil over the spuds (no need to go near the sausages) and season these with salt and pepper. Sprinkle a few chopped herbs over everything and put on the middle shelf of the oven.

In the meantime, using a sharp knife, cut a circle into the skin a third of the way down each cored apple. This will prevent them from exploding when they cook.

After about 15 minutes remove the dish from the oven, turn all but 2 sausages so that the underside can brown, and then using tongs, insert a sausage into each apple. Put the dish back into the oven and continue cooking for another 30 minutes. You want the sausages to be nice and brown all over and the apples soft all the way through.

Apart from the bonus potatoes, my evening trip to the veggie plot produced a good bowl of French beans, a fine bunch of carrots, a couple of courgettes and some parsley. I cooked the beans French fashion for about 10–15 minutes (we only eat them with a crunch if they are to be added cold to a salad), drained them and tossed them in some butter, crushed garlic and the parsley. The other vegetables were steamed altogether in the same pan. Finally, I added a splosh of boiling water to the sausage dish, scraping the caramelised juices to make a small amount of gravy. It proved a huge success.

JULY 26TH *Had a great time at the boot fair down the lane this morning and bought all sorts of treasures including a fully working retro Roberts radio and a collection of pretty art nouveau porcelain. It comprised seven dinner plates, large meat platter, small oval platter, another bowl, dish, gravy/sauce boat, all without a single chip or crack for a tenner and was delivered personally to the door before lunch by Malcolm, the stallholder.*

JULY 27TH

I am guaranteeing rain by giving the vegetables a really long drink soaking the ground where the peas had been before adding some compost so that I can sow some more seeds this evening. I'm not sure what, but it will probably be another row of carrots, beetroot and fennel although, if history repeats itself, the latter will bolt before it bulks up if the weather is too hot. The Swiss chard is already producing flowers so I shall sow another batch, which will take us through to next spring. Because it has been so dry today I lifted the shallots and the red onions, laying them out in the greenhouse just in case the unpredictable weather turns to rain again.

JULY 28TH

Courgette and tomato bake

INGREDIENTS

225g (8oz) courgettes
1 tbsp plain flour
1 egg
½ tub crème fraîche (1 cup)
85g (3oz) cheese (Cheddar, Emmental, Gruyère – whatever you have in the fridge, or a mixture of these), grated
salt and ground black pepper
6 spring onions, sliced
2 tomatoes, chopped
1 egg
lots of fresh flat-leafed parsley, chopped (about 3 tbsp)

Preheat the oven to 200°C (180°C fan) mark 6. Grate the courgettes into a bowl. Put the flour into a separate bowl and break in the egg. Mix and add the crème fraîche and cheese, then season. Add to the courgettes with the remaining ingredients, stir, then pour into a shallow baking dish. Bake in the oven for about 30 minutes, or until golden brown and bubbling. Serve with a green salad.

NOTE

This works equally well if you double the quantities for four.

right: *Courgette and tomato bake*

This is like an onion pizza but with a flaky pastry.

Pissaladière

Put the onions into a frying pan with a good splash of olive oil and 1 cup water. Bring to the boil, stir, reduce the heat and simmer, stirring constantly, for 15–20 minutes until the water has evaporated and the onions are soft but not brown. Remove from the heat to cool.

Preheat the oven to 200°C (180°C fan) mark 6. Roll out the pastry on a lightly floured surface into a rectangle and place on a non-stick baking tray or a tray lined with baking parchment. Prick with a fork then, with a pointed knife, mark a 'frame' around the edge but without completely cutting through. Spread the cooled onions within the 'frame' and decorate with some of the anchovies (cut in two if large) making a criss-cross pattern. Place an olive in the middle of each diamond and sprinkle over the chopped herbs. Add a few grinds of pepper and a drizzle of olive oil. The anchovies will provide plenty of salt. Bake in the oven for about 30 minutes, or until the pastry is cooked through. Serve at room temperature with a green salad. This is great picnic food.

INGREDIENTS

- 4–5 large onions (red or white), finely sliced
- olive oil
- 1 standard pack of all butter flaky pastry
- 1 standard jar of anchovies, drained
- 1 small can pitted black olives, drained
- fresh herbs, such as thyme, oregano and basil
- ground black pepper

above: *Oops! A slightly overdone pissaladière, but tasty none the less*
left: *Ready to go into the oven*

JULY 30TH *We have ordered doors and windows for the hut, measurements taken for the flooring and outer timbers, and the wheels have been cleaned and painted black. My father was in the Royal Navy Volunteer Reserve during WW2 and was posted to Normandy. He was at Sword Beach for the D-Day landings and in one letter home to his father he wrote:*

> Dearest Folks,
> I wish I could say that the elements in this part of the world are being kind to us. They continue to vent their spleen in no uncertain manner. I now have a very warm girl sharing my cabin by the name of Beatrice. She and I spend most evenings together. Her company is excellent as she speaks not at all. In other words, I have wrangled a paraffin stove and life has already a brighter aspect.

Dad brought Beatrice home to Sussex after the War where she continued to do a very efficient job heating the workshop so that we could dubbin football boots in comfort. She now lives with me and will carry on the good work in the hut once it is completed.

top: *Dad's sketch with Beatrice in his tent in Normandy*
bottom: *Beatrice*
right: *Beginning to take shape*

JULY 31ST

I am sure that the fantastic abundance of fruit is thanks to the bees - we have never before had branches breaking from sheer weight.

Yesterday I was taken by a friend to choose two point-of-lay pullets, who I had already named Pauline and Hilary, to join our little flock of three girls. I was warned that it can be difficult to introduce new birds into an existing group. The secret apparently is to keep the newbies separate from the old ones, but somewhere close so they can observe each other. Bedtime was more problematic but having kept Sandra, Ann and Haynsie (the original trio) in their outer run I managed to coax Pauline and Hilary into the coop. Since the other three insist on sleeping on the roof regardless of the weather, I knew there would be no pillow fights. This morning I encouraged the matriarchs into their run, shut the gate and let out the pullets who appeared none the worse for wear but remained reluctant to leave the shady area except to nibble a bit of grass and drink. Later in the day they were full of beans and it was noticeable that Pauline is the dominant girl.

above: *Ripening on the tree*
left: *The girls having a dust bath at the spa*

Courgette patties

INGREDIENTS

- 3 courgettes (Cumberland sausage size rather than chipolata)
- 1 tbsp fresh flat-leafed parsley, chopped
- 1 tbsp fresh mint, chopped
- 1 tsp hot paprika
- 1 tbsp plain flour, plus extra to coat
- good pinch of salt and ground black pepper
- 2–3 spring onions, finely sliced
- ⅓–½ standard pack of feta cheese, roughly crumbled
- 1 egg
- small amount of vegetable oil to fry

Begin by coarsely grating the courgettes onto a clean tea towel then squeeze out as much moisture as you can.

Put the grated courgette into a bowl and add all the other ingredients apart from the oil. Mix thoroughly. Take a heaped tbsp of courgette mix and shape roughly into a ball, passing it from palm to palm. The mixture will be quite soft and sloppy but don't worry – because of this it's easier to pick up the flour from the dish and dust the patty in your hand, turning it and adding more flour so that it's well coated. Put to one side in a dish and continue making the patties until you have finished using the mixture. This amount should make six and either feed three people or two hungry ones.

Heat a shallow non-stick frying pan with a splash of oil over a moderate heat. Carefully lower the patties, flattening them with your spatula or fish slice until they are a good 1cm (½in) thick. Fry for at least 5 minutes, then flip over and cook for a further 3–5 minutes until golden brown.

left: *Veggie heaven*

Updated recipe for courgette patties

Add the following ingredients to the patty mixture:

- *canned kidney beans or chickpeas*
- *a pinch of ground cumin*
- *a pinch of ground turmeric*
- *a pinch of ground coriander*
- *fresh coriander, chopped*

We made a real meal of these serving them with the following side dishes: cooked beetroot, sliced and splashed with a little cider vinegar, a big bowl of lettuce, French beans cooked but with a little crunch in a dish with a few sliced spring onions, and 1 hard-boiled egg per person cut into quarters

Make a light vinaigrette from the oil of your choice, red, white wine or cider vinegar, a little Dijon mustard and salt and ground black pepper. Pour this over the French beans, etc. and serve everything with some crusty bread (warmed in the oven) torn into chunks.

–

A vicious flu bug has kept me confined to bed for a full two weeks and I have lost time in the garden, so in order to catch up I have overcome the problem by buying a packet of growing salad leaves at the supermarket. They don't need to be separated into individual seedlings, simply tease apart into little clumps and put in the ground. Keep them watered and they will reward you in record time with a regular supply of young, cut-and-come again leaves.

Plagued by a whitefly infestation in the greenhouse, the bane of gardeners, I bought a tray of French marigolds to plant in front of the tomato plants in the hope that the scent they give off will deter the insects, but they too are faced with a problem since slugs and particularly snails love them. Every year I purchase yet more dahlia tubers starting them off in flowerpots in the greenhouse and, when the frosts are over, find a suitable space in the borders. This year, for a change, I made room in the raised beds in the veg plot; the reason being that they would be looked after, watered, occasionally fed and picked regularly for the house.

top: *Growing salad leaves*
bottom: *Fighting the whitefly*

I went to check up on the chickens yesterday afternoon. Haynsie (named after Johnny because, being a light Sussex and black and white, she 'wears' Fulham's colours) has become increasingly broody and I have to keep on removing her from the nesting box. Usually a cheery girl, she doesn't like the upheaval one jot and snaps at me, but it's the only way to stop her.

The cultivated blackberries, which originated in my mother's garden are beginning to ripen and, since they are only fifty yards away from the hives, the bees have certainly been doing their stuff. There were plenty to pick for a pudding for supper.

Blackberry sponge pudding

INGREDIENTS

450g (1lb) blackberries
55g (2oz) caster sugar, plus extra to sprinkle over the fruit
55g (2 oz) self-raising flour
1 egg
55g (2oz) butter, very soft
finely grated zest and juice of ½ lemon

Preheat the oven to 200°C (180°C fan) mark 6. Wash and drain the blackberries, then put them into a medium shallow ovenproof dish and dust with the sugar for sprinkling.

In a bowl, mix together the flour, egg, butter and the 55g (2oz) sugar with a wooden spoon until it's a smooth cream. Add the lemon juice and zest and mix in. Spread roughly over the blackberries and bake in the oven for about 20–30 minutes until it is bubbling and the top is brown. Serve warm or at room temperature with lots of cream or custard (see right).

right: *Blackbugs galore*

Custard

INGREDIENTS

1¼ cups milk (whole milk is nicer)
sugar, to taste
2 egg yolks (don't waste the whites – make some meringues)
2 level tsp cornflour
1 tsp vanilla extract
sugar to taste
vanilla extract

Warm the milk with the sugar in a non-stick pan until it is just coming up to the boil. In a separate bowl, beat the egg yolks into the cornflour and add the vanilla extract.

Remove the milk and sugar mix from the heat and pour a very little amount into the egg mixture, stirring quickly. Then add a little more, stirring all the while. This will heat the eggs without cooking them. Next, pass the egg mixture through a small sieve into the warm milk, stirring as you go. Put back on to a moderate heat, whisking all the while to prevent the custard from curdling. It will thicken quite quickly (because of the cornflour). The moment it begins to boil and the custard coats the back of the spoon remove from the heat immediately.

Meringues

INGREDIENTS

2 egg whites
4 tbsp caster sugar

Preheat the oven to 110°C (100°C fan) mark ¼. Cover a baking sheet with baking parchment. Whisk the egg whites in a very clean, grease-free bowl until you have nice stiff, glossy peaks, then gradually whisk in the caster sugar, one spoon at a time. Using a tablespoon, place dollops onto the prepared sheet and bake in the oven until they are just beginning to take on a little colour and are nice and hollow when you tap them. Store in an airtight tin until needed.

top: *Clever girls*
bottom: *Hilary*

above: *Autumn in the air*

What a windy night... barrow loads of apples on the grass much to the delight of the residents from Watership Down; *pots blown over; the scent of autumn is in the air.*

AUG 2ND

Sunday lunch is a wonderful invention, to be enjoyed at leisure in good company. However, by the evening I often feel deflated emotionally and inflated physically – not an ideal combination, but if there is any room left, a light supper is on the cards. It could be a BLT and a cuppa, or scrambled eggs with chives on buttered toast, or even baked beans and a tumbler of ice-cold milk.

This Sunday when I was watering the vegetables I found lurking under the leaves a large courgette, which I picked along with some chard.

Chard and courgette gratin

INGREDIENTS

- 1 large courgette, cut lengthways into 5mm (¼in) slices
- 1 garlic clove, chopped
- salt and ground black pepper
- butter
- 1 bunch of Swiss chard (or large bag of spinach), roughly chopped
- 1 tbsp plain flour
- 1 egg
- 55–85g (2–3oz) grated cheese (I usually use a mix of Gruyère and Emmental)
- 2–3 tbsp crème fraîche
- 1 extra egg per person

Preheat the oven to 200°C (180°C fan) mark 6. Lay the courgette slices in a baking dish, then scatter the chopped garlic on top. Season and add a few dots of butter before baking it in the oven for 20 minutes.

Cook the chard or spinach quickly in very little water, drain and squeeze out as much liquid as possible, then spread it on top of the courgette, mix together the flour, egg, cheese and crème fraîche and spread it over the vegetables. Return to the oven for about 5 minutes, or until it is beginning to brown. Take it out of the oven again and make little nests in the mixture, then crack in an extra egg per person. Put it back in the oven for a further 5 minutes until it is bubbling, the whites cooked and the yolks still runny.

AUG 3RD

I spent a wonderful, giggly Monday with five old friends. I dread to calculate the combined ages, but from the topics of conversation to the constant laughter, we were back to being at school. It was bliss. We sat in the shade in a lovely garden and Julia did us proud with this tasty all-in-one chicken bake.

All-in-one chicken bake

INGREDIENTS

1 piece of skin-on chicken per person, such as drumsticks, thighs or breast
½ butternut squash (skin on or off), sliced or cut into chunks
several red onions, cut into quarters
1 whole garlic bulb, cut in half
fresh herbs, such as basil, parsley, oregano or 1 tsp dried mixed herbs
¾ cup olive oil
salt and ground black pepper

Preheat the oven to 200°C (180°C fan) mark 6. Place the chicken pieces, skin side up, in a roasting pan along with the butternut squash, onions and garlic. Scatter over the herbs and drizzle over the olive oil. Season well and bake in the oven for 40–45 minutes until the chicken juices run clear.

Julia's pudding was another delight...

above: *Summer bouquet*
below: *Dina and Julia in the haha, St. Michael's Burton Park, 1966*

top: *A welcome friend to the garden*
bottom: *Trug of grapes*

Chilled mango pudding

INGREDIENTS
1 mango big enough for 2 people
1 cup full fat Greek yogurt
½ small tub crème fraîche
4 heaped tsp dark brown muscovado sugar

Peel the mango with a vegetable peeler, then simply cut slices from the fruit around the central stone and put into a pretty glass bowl. Lightly whisk the yogurt and crème fraîche together with a fork and spoon over the fruit. Dust with the muscovado sugar. This will be quite clumpy but it will gradually even out as it melts. Leave to chill for at least an hour, preferably more.

TIP
For a lighter version whisk some 0% fat Greek yogurt (about 3 heaped tbsp) with the same amount of crème fraîche. Light muscovado sugar is fine but the dark gives greater depth of flavour. You could do this with almost any fruit: peaches, cooked plums, nectarines, etc. and, if put into small ramekins, covered with a sprinkle of sugar and popped under a hot grill for a minute or two, you will get a kind of crème brûlée.

Grape pud

INGREDIENTS
1 bunch of sweet, seedless green or red grapes (enough to fill a small bowl to serve 1–2 people)
double cream (enough to serve 1–2 people)
demerara sugar (enough for 1–2 people)

This is similar to the above but naughtier. Halve the grapes and put into a pretty bowl. Whip the cream with a whisk until it's the consistency of shaving foam and pour over the grapes. Dust liberally with demerara sugar. Cover with clingfilm and keep in the fridge for a few hours. It's another wonderful, light summer pudding.

This is our Christmas and Easter standby. I never buy 'green' gammon, only smoked as it has more flavour and although the initial outlay is fairly hefty, there is absolutely no waste, as it is a meal which keeps on giving.

above: *More than 5-a-day and counting*

Boiled smoked gammon

INGREDIENTS

1 piece smoked British gammon (the size is up to you. This can be quite salty so don't add any to the pan when cooking)
2 onions
2 leeks, cut into chunks
2 carrots, cut into chunks
2 celery sticks, cut into pieces
450g (1lb) potatoes, peeled
2 bay leaves
1 tsp black peppercorns

Put the gammon, vegetables, bay leaves and black peppercorns into a large pan, cover with water and bring to the boil. Reduce the heat and simmer until you can pull the skin away with tongs. A small piece would only take about 30 minutes, a large one longer. Either serve hot or cold but remember that if you leave it in the pan to cool, it will continue to cook for a while afterwards. Remove the rind before serving. As all the vegetables have been cooked with the ham, when serving, lift them from the pan with a slotted spoon on to a platter and cover with the parsley sauce.

Parsley sauce

INGREDIENTS

1 tbsp plain flour
30g (1oz) butter
1 cup warm ham stock (from cooking the ham)
1 cup milk
2 tbsp fresh parsley, chopped
salt and ground black pepper

Melt the butter and stir in the flour in a non-stick pan over a moderate heat. Cook for a minute before adding the warm stock, whisking well to avoid lumps. Add the milk and bring to the boil, stirring all the while. Allow to bubble for a minute, then add the parsley, some ground pepper and taste. Add more salt, if necessary.

TIP

Cold meat can be cut into many more slices than if served hot. You will also be left with a lot of tasty ham stock. Don't waste this but use it as a base for lentil soup (see page 68). However, before you go ahead taste the stock because it can be too salty, in which case, dilute it with more water.

top: *Ma's egg and bacon pie*
bottom: *my brothers Neil and Paul, Dad and me on Southwold beach, 1959*

Ma's open egg and bacon pie

INGREDIENTS

1 standard pack of all butter shortcrust pastry (if you have any trimmings leftover, then make a couple of jam tarts or feed to the birds as they love the fat content, especially in winter)
leftover cold gammon (see page 67), chopped, or several rashers of smoked streaky or back bacon
1–2 large tomatoes, finely sliced
1 egg per person
a little full-fat milk
salt and ground black pepper
1 tbsp fresh parsley, chopped
1 tbsp fresh chives, chopped

Preheat the oven to 200°C (180°C fan) mark 6. Line a 25cm/10in flan ring with the pastry, prick with a fork, then lay a piece of baking parchment on top and fill with either ceramic beads made for the job or, as I do, dried butter beans. Bake in the oven for about 10 minutes, then remove the beads/beans (they will be hot) and parchment and cook a further five minutes. Remove from the oven and allow to cool slightly before placing the chopped gammon or bacon rashers on the bottom followed by the finely sliced tomatoes. Make four or five little nests and drop a raw egg into each one. Pour on a little milk, season well and sprinkle with chopped parsley and chives. Bake for about 30–40 minutes until the eggs are set and the bacon is cooked. I can smell and taste it now, so strong are the memories of eating this huddled behind the windbreak after a swim in the North Sea at Southwold.

Ham and lentil soup

INGREDIENTS

leftover vegetables (see method)
2½ cups ham stock (from cooking gammon on page 67)
1 cup red lentils
1–2 cups milk

If the stock is not too salty and you have any of the vegetables and parsley sauce left over from cooking the gammon, add these to a pan with the stock and lentils. Stir and bring to the boil. Reduce the heat and simmer gently until the lentils are cooked, then whizz with a hand-held blender. Add the milk, whizz again and check for seasoning. This freezes well.

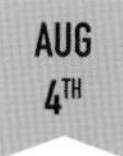
AUG 4TH

This is groundbreaking news and the result of months of research: lose weight and you stop snoring. You read it here first.

Turkey escalopes

INGREDIENTS

vegetable or sunflower oil to fry
1 Romano red pepper cut in half, deseeded and finely sliced
1 banana shallot, finely sliced
1 fat garlic clove, crushed
2 turkey escalopes
1 glass of white wine
½ small tub crème fraîche
1 tsp sweet smoked paprika
salt and ground black pepper

Heat a little oil in a frying pan over a moderate heat and tip in the pepper and shallot. Stir and cook for 2–3 minutes before adding the garlic then add the escalopes. Cook for 2 minutes, then add the wine. Turn the escalopes over and cook a further 2 minutes before adding the crème fraîche and paprika. Simmer for another minute or so, then season. Serve immediately with rice, pasta, couscous or mashed potato and something green.

below: *Peaches straight from the tree*

AUG 9TH

For the last two days, I have mixed the new girls with the elder ladies and so far, so good. They tend to keep to themselves, albeit in the same run but I haven't witnessed any nasty spats. The adjustment has been really quick and the acid test will be when they all start laying again – we haven't had any eggs now for over a week.

The grapes have ripened and I bottled the peaches so that we can enjoy them when the frosts come. What a dreadful thought.

AUG 10TH

What a wake-up call the last few days have been... rain, cloudy skies, cool mornings – even the robins have started to sing differently and are sounding quite wintery. However, the blackberries are firing on all cylinders and it's a case of getting to the end of the row and having to start again at the beginning to keep up with them. I decided to make a blackberry jelly for pudding, using the recipe on the back of the packet of leaf gelatine to get the proper quantities.

Bramble jelly

INGREDIENTS

- blackberries (see method for weight)
- jam sugar with added pectin (see method for weight)
- juice of 1 lemon
- a knob of butter

I always include a few unripe fruits to increase the pectin level – this is what makes the jelly set. Don't bother to weigh the raw fruit, merely rinse it thoroughly under a cold tap and put in a deep pan with a little water and bring to the boil. Stir and mash the fruit and cook for 5–6 minutes.

Strain into a bowl through a piece of muslin or jelly bag and, when cold enough to handle, squeeze to extract the remaining juice. Measure the liquid and for each 600ml (1 pint) add 450g (1lb) sugar plus the juice of a lemon. Heat the juice and add the sugar, stirring until it dissolves. Bring to the boil, then add a knob of butter. Wait until the temperature reaches setting point (220°C/440°F) then pour it carefully into hot sterilised jars (see page 5) and seal immediately. Don't forget to label when cold or it could be mistaken for blackcurrant jelly.

above: *Storm clouds over Sussex*
right: *Blackberry jelly mould*

Supper tonight: freshly dug Pink Fir Apple spuds steamed over mint, first pickings of runner beans (from the two plants left alone – so far – by Peter Rabbit), black Tuscan kale and raspberries with oodles of cream.

Ma's lemon drizzle cake

INGREDIENTS

175g (6oz) unsalted butter
175g (6oz) self-raising flour
175g (6oz) caster sugar
2 eggs
a small pinch of salt

FOR THE TOPPING

finely grated zest and juice of 1 unwaxed lemon
115g (4oz) caster sugar

Preheat the oven to 200°C (180°C fan) mark 6. Grease a Swiss roll tin or similar small shallow roasting dish. Melt the butter, take off the heat and add to the other ingredients, beating so there are no lumps. Pour into the prepared dish and bake in the oven for 20–30 minutes until risen, golden brown and a skewer or knife comes out clean.

For the topping, mix the lemon zest and juice with the caster sugar and pour over the cooked cake. Leave to cool before cutting into rectangular slices.

TIPS

- *If you have them in your store cupboard add a tablespoon of poppy seeds to the cake mix and, instead of using sugar to drizzle on the cooked cake, why not try some runny honey mixed with the lemon juice?*
- *Lemon drizzle cake doubles up as a pudding if served with some fresh raspberries or strawberries and vanilla ice cream.*

above: *A crock of gold*
left: *Ma's lemon drizzle cake*

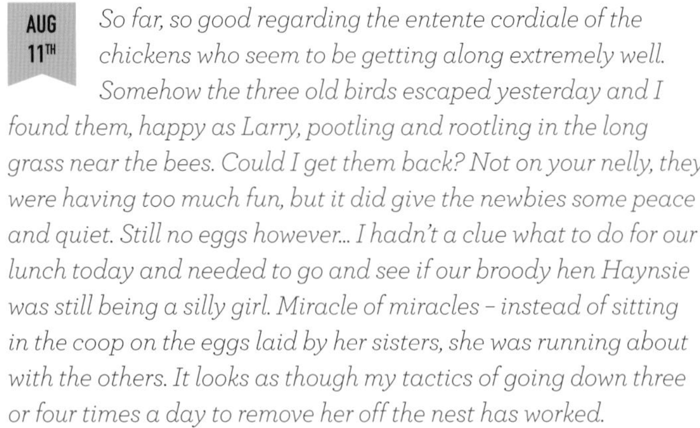

AUG 11TH *So far, so good regarding the entente cordiale of the chickens who seem to be getting along extremely well. Somehow the three old birds escaped yesterday and I found them, happy as Larry, pootling and rootling in the long grass near the bees. Could I get them back? Not on your nelly, they were having too much fun, but it did give the newbies some peace and quiet. Still no eggs however... I hadn't a clue what to do for our lunch today and needed to go and see if our broody hen Haynsie was still being a silly girl. Miracle of miracles – instead of sitting in the coop on the eggs laid by her sisters, she was running about with the others. It looks as though my tactics of going down three or four times a day to remove her off the nest has worked.*

AUG 12TH *I have just collected our first pullet's egg – no larger than a ping-pong ball and nut brown. Wonders will never cease as when I had a peek in the temporary hutch (in case the newcomers were reluctant to use the existing coop) constructed from an old kitchen cabinet, I found four perfectly formed white eggs – must be Haynsie's. Up until now she has been a lazy layer, producing odd, torpedo-shaped eggs only when she felt inclined, but they are definitely hers. Things are beginning to look promising.*

Yesterday, when I was in the village, I moved to one side on the narrow pavement to let two old girls by who were walking arm in arm. They were charming and thanked me profusely, to which I replied, 'I shall get my reward in heaven.' One turned and said, 'My dear, heaven is for climate, hell is for sociability.'

above: *Eyeing up the competition*
below: *Young sparrowhawk with its prey*

AUG 13TH *As I was about to put some stuff in the recycling bin a scuffling under the trees caught my attention: a sparrowhawk was staring at me with a dead pigeon in its talons. He didn't seem at all perturbed so I ran inside to grab my camera. When I returned he was still there and I took this picture from less than four feet away. Apparently, the presence of sparrowhawks means that the environment is particularly clean.*

Russian salad

INGREDIENTS

1 tbsp natural yogurt
1 tbsp good-quality mayonnaise
a couple of splashes of balsamic vinegar
1 hard-boiled egg per person, cut into quarters plus a combination of any of the following:
cooked baby turnips, chopped into small cubes
raw fennel, sliced and chopped
2 small carrots, cooked and cut into cubes
a few new potatoes, steamed, peeled and cut into cubes
1 cup either cooked (fresh or frozen) petits pois or garden peas
1 bunch of radishes, sliced
1 green pepper, deseeded and finely chopped
1 red onion, finely chopped
some fresh parsley, chopped
a little fresh basil, torn at the last moment, not chopped
2 tomatoes, cut into small pieces
1 cucumber either finely sliced or cut into cubes
1 avocado, peeled, stoned and sliced

Mix the yogurt and mayonnaise with a little balsamic vinegar and drizzle over the selection of vegetables and egg. Best enjoyed sitting in the sun with a friend, four footed or otherwise.

below: *Russian salad*

I am always on the look out for different pickles and chutneys since over the years my tooth has become sweeter, and I tend now to spurn the sharper recipes. At this time of year Jimmy is on full time apple duty, collecting the damaged windfalls into a pile for the compost heap, and saving good ones for the kitchen. This summer the outdoor cucumbers have been prolific and with no hint of bitterness. I grew three plants of the Burpless variety and I am finding it difficult to cope with the crop. This is a brilliant way of using two gluts in one:

Apple and cucumber chutney

INGREDIENTS

- 900g (2lb) cucumbers
- 225g (8oz) onions (I used a red onion), finely sliced
- 2½ cups vinegar (I used white wine vinegar but you could always use red wine, cider or malt but bear in mind the flavour will change)
- 900g (2lb) apples (I used a mixture of eaters and cookers)
- 450g (1lb) demerara sugar
- 1 tsp salt
- 1 tsp cayenne pepper

below: *From plot to pot*

Begin by putting your clean jars into a warmed oven to sterilise (see page 5). Next, peel the cucumbers. A quick way to turn them into tiny chunks is as follows: hold the cucumber in your left hand and then cut into the flesh lengthways to about 10cm (4in), then do the same at right angles to the first cuts. Put the cucumber on to a board and slice through it – the little chunks will fall off. Continue on down the cucumber until you have cut it all up, then put the chunks into a stainless steel pan.

Add the onions to the cucumber and pour on the vinegar.

Add the apples, then put the pan on the heat and bring to the boil. Reduce the heat and cook gently until everything is soft, stirring every now and again – this could take 15–20 minutes. Add the sugar, salt and cayenne. Stir and bring to the boil. A word of warning: you need to cook this for at least 30 minutes, maybe more until it thickens, but the hotter and less runny it becomes will mean that it will spit at you when you stir – and you must stir frequently to prevent the bottom from burning. To avoid accidents, place one of those anti-splatter contraptions over the pan lifting it enough to put a wooden spoon underneath when you stir. When it is thick but still slightly sloppy, pour carefully into your sterilised jars. Seal and store for a month in a cool, dark place before eating.

TIP

This is a quick way to prepare a lot of apples for a pie or chutney: peel the whole fruit with a vegetable peeler, then using a knife, cut into the flesh in a random, criss-cross way. Slice the fruit through almost to the core – once again, the little pieces will fall off. Far easier than having to peel, core and slice. Add the fruit as you go into the pan and stir – the vinegar will stop the apple from going brown.

AUG 14TH

Out of the blue I was suddenly cooking lunch for eight, so last night, I took two free-range ducklings out of the freezer. This morning I removed the giblets to make stock for the gravy, reserving the livers to make a little pâté.

Quick duck liver pâté

INGREDIENTS

liver(s) from the duckling(s)
1–2 slices pancetta per liver
1 garlic clove, crushed
1 small shallot, finely chopped
2–3 fresh thyme sprigs, leaves picked
salt and ground black pepper
15–30g (½–1oz) butter

Rinse the liver(s) and place on a board, then take hold of a piece and run the knife across the liver(s), gently scraping the flesh in order to remove any stringy, sinewy bits. Put to one side.

Heat a small frying pan over a moderate heat and add the pancetta, garlic and shallot. Stir from time to time until the shallot is soft and the pancetta cooked but not crispy. Add the liver(s) and stir. Add the thyme and season with a little salt and pepper. The liver(s) will only take a minute or two to cook. Remove from the heat and allow to cool before putting into a small blender (or into a container and use a hand-held blender). Blitz until smooth, then press into a small dish or ramekin. Leave to one side to cool.

Once the pâté is cold, melt a little butter and pour this on top. Put into the fridge for 2–3 hours until it is firm and thoroughly chilled. Serve on little toasts or, as I did, oatcakes with a dish of cornichons (baby gherkins).

above: *Duck liver* pâté
left: *The rambling rose in the apple tree*

above: *Mixed courgette, red onion and tomato bake to accompany Roast duckling*

Roast duckling with veg

INGREDIENTS

1 celery stick, cut into chunks
1 large onion, cut into pieces
1 fresh duckling
1 apple, cut into quarters
1 orange, cut into quarters
2–3 garlic cloves, crushed (with skin on)
salt and ground black pepper
1 cup chicken or vegetable stock

ACCOMPANYING VEGETABLES

new potatoes,steamed on a bed of fresh mint
courgettes, sliced
red onions, finely sliced
tomatoes, sliced
fresh mint, thyme and parsley sprigs
butter or olive oil
chard
juice of ½ lemon

Preheat the oven to 200°C (180°C fan) mark 6. First into the roasting pan went the celery and onion along with the neck, gizzard and heart of the duckling. These will cook down and make a wonderful base for gravy. Then I inserted the apple and orange pieces and garlic into the cavity of the duckling. I sprinkled the bird generously with salt and pepper and put in the middle of the oven to cook for about 1½–1¾ hours until the skin was a deep golden brown and the juices ran clear.

I lifted the duck on to a serving dish and covered it with foil and a couple of clean cloths to keep it warm while I made the gravy. I drained off as much of the fat from the pan as possible, keeping it for another occasion when I may want to roast potatoes, and added the stock (or you can use water) and cooked the gravy on the stove, scraping up all the gooey bits from the bottom of the pan. I poured the gravy into a little jug.

Halfway through cooking the duck, I prepared the vegetables and laid them neatly in a shallow dish with the herbs, seasoned them well, dotted them with butter (or you can drizzle them with a little olive oil), then covered with foil. I didn't add any garlic as there was enough in the ducklings and I put it into the hot oven to bake for about 20 minutes before removing the foil and cooking for another 10–15 minutes. This is a lovely way to cook vegetables because they don't disintegrate into a mush and you can really taste their individual flavours. As an extra, I cooked some chard in a pan with a dash of water and some salt for about 5 minutes. Drained, then cut it up roughly with a knife adding a little lemon juice and butter.

I picked a large bowl of beautiful raspberries, which had by no means suffered from the drenching downfalls of rain we have been experiencing recently.

Raspberry meringue

INGREDIENTS

4 egg whites (keep the yolks to add to a couple of whole eggs and make some scrambled eggs or an omelette)
225g (8oz) caster sugar
1¼ cups double cream
1 standard punnet of raspberries
a little icing sugar

Preheat the oven to 180°C (160°C fan) mark 4. Take a piece of baking parchment to fit your baking tray and scrunch it up, then unravel it and place on the tray – by doing this it will keep flat.

In a very clean bowl, whisk the egg whites with electric beaters until they are nice and stiff and form peaks – don't whisk them at full throttle, but one or two notches under the max. Add the sugar, little by little, whisking all the time until it is all incorporated. Spread the meringue mixture onto the parchment in a square shape, about 4cm (1½in) deep and place in the middle shelf of the oven and cook for about 15 minutes, or until the top is turning golden. Remove from the heat and allow to cool a moment or two. Next, flip it over on to a serving dish and gently peel off the parchment. Cover with a clean cloth and leave to get completely cold.

When ready to serve, whip the cream until it holds its shape and spread over half the square. Tumble on top a few handfuls of raspberries and gently fold over the other half of the meringue. Dust with icing sugar using a sieve and scatter the remaining raspberries around it. You could ring the changes with any other fruit.

left: *Raspberry meringue*

above: *Tomatoes ripening on the vine*

AUG 15TH

After over a decade of blight affecting the tomato crop, this year it looks as though I might have escaped. I am growing Green Zebra, Black Cherry, Brandyboy, Marmande, Sungold and some Italian ones for pasta sauces. I love gazpacho (chilled tomato soup), as it reminds me of happy holidays with Jimmy in Spain.

Gazpacho

INGREDIENTS

450g (1lb) ripe tomatoes
1 celery stick
4 spring onions
1 green pepper
1 small cucumber or ½ large one
2 garlic cloves
½ cup olive oil, plus extra to drizzle
salt and ground black pepper
a dash of red wine vinegar

Take each tomato and make a shallow cut with a knife – this will make it easier to remove the skin. Put in a heatproof bowl and cover with boiling water. Leave for 2 minutes, drain and run under the cold tap to cool. Peel away the skins and roughly chop the tomatoes. Cut the celery and spring onions into chunks, remove the seeds from the pepper and tear into pieces. Peel the cucumber and chop roughly and peel the garlic. Put everything into a blender with the olive oil and blitz until smooth. Season and add a dash of red wine vinegar. Taste and, if a little too thick, add some water to slacken. Pour into a container, seal and leave overnight in the fridge to chill thoroughly.

Serve with a drizzle of olive oil and garlic croutons (see page 235). In some restaurants in Spain you are given a side dish of extra vegetables, chopped very finely – even hard-boiled egg – which you spoon into the soup.

NOTE

Many recipes include stale bread, but I prefer it without.

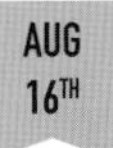

Cherry and raspberry bake

INGREDIENTS

225g (8oz) cherries, stoned
1 standard punnet or bowl of raspberries
1 egg
1 heaped tbsp self-raising flour
4 heaped tsp crème fraîche
1 cup full-fat milk
1 heaped tbsp caster sugar or to taste
caster or icing sugar to sprinkle

Preheat the oven to 200°C (180°C fan) mark 6. Lay the cherries on the bottom of a buttered shallow baking dish and scatter on the raspberries. Beat the egg with the flour, crème fraîche, milk and enough sugar to taste. Whisk to remove any lumps, then pour over the fruit. Bake in the oven until puffed up and golden. Sprinkle with a little more caster sugar or dust with icing sugar and serve warm or at room temperature with cream.

above: *Cherry and raspberry bake*
below: *Spaghetti courgetti*

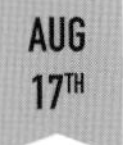

Spaghetti courgetti

INGREDIENTS

4 ripe tomatoes, chopped (no need to skin or remove the seeds) or 400g (14oz) can chopped tomatoes
1–2 garlic cloves, crushed
2 tbsp olive oil
¼ tsp sugar
salt and ground black pepper
40% dried spaghetti to 60% spiralised courgettes
grated Parmesan cheese
fresh basil leaves

Make the sauce by putting the tomatoes, garlic, olive oil and sugar into a pan, bring it to the boil, then reduce the heat and simmer gently, stirring every now and again to prevent it burning. Season with salt and pepper.

In the meantime, put a large pan filled with water on to heat. Using your spiraliser, prepare the courgettes and, when the water is boiling, add the pasta. Five minutes before the end of cooking add the courgettes. Drain and tip into the tomato sauce. Mix well and serve with lots of freshly grated Parmesan, a drizzle of olive oil and basil leaves.

above: *Nest of egg noodles, ginger and garlic*

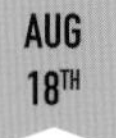

AUG 18TH

Giant prawns and stir-fry veg

INGREDIENTS

1 pack of fresh, shell-on king prawns, enough for 2 people
2.5cm (1in) piece fresh root ginger, peeled and grated
2–3 cloves garlic cloves, crushed (skin on)
1 fresh red chilli, chopped (I like to keep the seeds for extra heat)
juice of 1 lemon
1 tbsp soy sauce
450g (1lb) broad beans in their pods
1 tbsp vegetable oil
1 bunch of asparagus, the ends removed and sliced finely on the diagonal (it looks prettier)
1 fennel bulb, very finely sliced
2 nests of dried egg noodles, cooked according to pack instructions or buy some ready prepared
a good handful of fresh coriander, chopped
toasted sesame oil

Prepare the prawns by removing the heads, tails, shells, legs, etc. Cut along the back with a sharp knife and remove the black intestinal vein. Rinse and place in a bowl with the ginger, garlic, chilli, lemon juice and soy. Leave to marinate in the fridge for at least an hour.

Shell the broad beans (see tip on page 23). Heat the vegetable oil in a wok over a high heat and add the prawns, stirring all the while until they turn pink. Remove with a slotted spoon and put to one side, keeping warm. Heat the wok again and add the vegetables. Stir-fry for about 5 minutes. Add the prawns to reheat, the cooked noodles and chopped coriander. Drizzle a tiny amount of toasted sesame oil and serve at once. A steaming pot of jasmine tea is a perfect drink.

TIP

Never cook with toasted sesame oil – only use it as a last minute flavouring.

AUG 19TH

We have a peach tree growing up against the south-facing barn wall and, although it was covered in blossom, the late frosts killed off most of it. However, on closer inspection I found a cluster of ripe peaches tucked away only a foot off the ground, hidden behind the blackcurrant bush – even the squirrels hadn't found them. I picked four and also a tiny bunch of grapes, which were more or less ripe from a bit of the vine, which had winkled its way through the window into the greenhouse.

Last night, unusually for us now that we are in our dotage and are in bed by 9.30 p.m., we had some friends from the village over for kitchen sups. She is a veggie and he is a self-confessed, very difficult person to please. The menu: roast chicken with tarragon, baked tomatoes with different basils, mixed courgettes with red onion and a cheese topping, new potatoes, a huge bowl of runner beans, stewed peaches and grapes and strawberry ice cream, which I prepared in advance.

top: *Squirrel Nutkin looking as though butter wouldn't melt...*
bottom: *Free-range chicken but definitely not for the pot!*

Roast chicken

INGREDIENTS

- 1 free-range chicken
- fresh tarragon (the amount is up to you, but use less tarragon than parsley as it's stronger)
- fresh parsley (the amount is up to you)
- 2 garlic cloves, crushed
- juice of 1–2 lemons
- 40g (1½oz) soft butter

Preheat the oven to 200°C (180°C fan) mark 6. Remove the elastic truss from the chicken. Roughly chop the tarragon and parsley. Place in a bowl and mix in the garlic, lemon juice and butter. Very carefully, using your fingers, gently ease under the skin on the breast of the chicken and very carefully (so as not to tear it) push in the buttery herby mixture.

Roast for about 1½ hours (check the weight of the chicken), or until the juices run clear. Stir a little boiling water into the juices in the tray and return to the heat for a few minutes. Once the chicken has rested for 10 minutes, either carve it as normal or, using kitchen scissors, first cut in half along the backbone, then into quarters removing the legs from the carcass, then everything once again. You will end up with eight pieces of chicken, all with lovely crispy skin. Place in a dish and pour over the tarragon juices. Serve with seasonal vegetables or a simple green salad.

above: *Ready to go in the oven*
below: *Raspberry ice cream*

Baked tomatoes

INGREDIENTS
450g (1lb) mixed, different coloured tomatoes, sliced
olive oil
salt and ground black pepper
juice of 1 lemon
fresh basil leaves

So far so good this year, in spite of the horrid weather we've been experiencing lately and there is (big 'touch wood') still no sign of blight on the tomato plants. I picked a lovely selection of Gardeners' delight, some teardrop-shaped teeny ones and the first pair of large beef Italian tomatoes. I cut the small ones in half and put them in the bottom of a dish, then sliced the large ones and positioned them on top in a line. I splashed on a good drizzle of olive oil, some salt and pepper, lots of lemon juice and plenty of basil. I happen to be growing several varieties of basil this year but any will do. Into the pre-heated oven it went to bake for about 25 minutes at 200°C (180°C fan) mark 6.

Raspberry ice cream

INGREDIENTS
450g (1lb) raspberries
150ml (¼ pint) double cream
juice of ½ lemon
caster sugar to taste (about 2 tbsp)

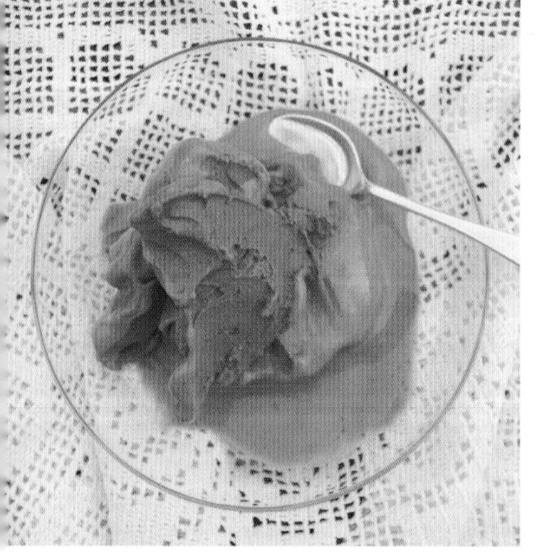

Put the raw raspberries into a blender and pass through a sieve to remove the pips. Very lightly whip the cream. Add the lemon juice to the raspberry purée and then pour it on to the sugar; doing it in this order, the sugar dissolves more quickly. Next, fold in the cream, then pour it into the ice-cream maker and follow the manufacturer's instructions.

The raspberry ice cream and stewed peaches and grapes were a huge hit. Our tricky to feed guest ate everything given to him and said that, had he been at home, he would have licked the plate. I'm happy with that.

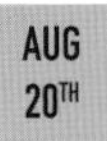

AUG 20TH

I have the room to grow different varieties of courgette but plain green ones taste just as good.

Mixed courgette gratin

INGREDIENTS

1 yellow courgette, sliced
1 green courgette, sliced
1 white patty pan squash, cut into wedges
1 red onion, sliced
a good handful of fresh flat-leafed parsley, torn not chopped
olive oil
salt and ground black pepper

FOR THE TOPPING

1 egg
1 tbsp plain or self-raising flour (if you use self-raising then you get a bit more of a puff)
1 small tub crème fraîche (I only had the tail end Charlie of a pot, about a dessertspoon, so made it up with some single cream)
85g (3oz) grated cheese (I used a mixture of Gruyère and Emmental but Cheddar is fine)
salt and ground black pepper

Preheat the oven to 200°C (180°C fan) mark 6. Place the courgettes and squash in a shallow gratin dish along with the onion and scatter with the torn parsley. Pour on a good drizzle of olive oil, salt and pepper and into the oven to bake for about 15 minutes.

To make the topping, whisk the egg and flour together to prevent lumps. Add the other ingredients and mix well. Scoop this over the vegetables and spread roughly – it doesn't matter if not everything is covered with the cheese sauce. Bake in the oven for about 10 minutes until it is bubbling and golden brown.

TIP *This looked and tasted absolutely gorgeous and would make a perfect light supper if accompanied by a baked potato.*

above: The hut in its original green overlooking the water meadow
below: Oven roasted tomatoes ready to be turned into soup

Progress on the hut is going in leaps and bounds. I decided that I wanted an old window at the towing end above the daybed and went back to the reclamation yard where I found a perfect one: the right proportions, with leaded stained glass. I clambered up the ladder to stand 'inside' the hut and couldn't believe how high off the ground it is. The view across the fields is going to be spectacular.

AUG 21ST

The tomatoes are ripening faster than I can pick them and to deal with the crop I made a batch of roasted tomato soup to put in the freezer for another day. It can also be used undiluted as a sauce for pasta or base for a pizza or Bolognese.

Concentrated roasted tomato soup

INGREDIENTS

It doesn't really matter what quantity you use but to 450g (1lb) tomatoes add:
1 large onion, quartered
2 celery sticks, cut into chunks
1 large carrot, chopped
2 garlic cloves, crushed
1 green or red chilli (seeds included if you want extra heat)
1 level tsp granulated sugar
good drizzle of olive oil
salt and ground black pepper
any fresh herbs, such as basil, parsley, thyme and/or oregano

Preheat the oven to 200°C (180°C fan) mark 6. Cut the tomatoes into quarters and put in a roasting dish with all the other ingredients. Bake in the oven until the vegetables are soft and just beginning to singe. Keep checking. Pass through a sieve and, when cold, freeze in small quantities – keep a few plastic butter containers for this purpose and when frozen, remove the tomato purée and put into bags so that you can reuse the tubs for something else.

NOTE

I have mentioned before, not to add garlic to anything you are freezing, particularly soup, as the flavour can change – add it when reheating.

AUG 22ND

Jimmy's collection of windfalls is rapidly taking over so I thought I had better get to grips with the riper ones. We love jellies of all kinds with meat and poultry and instead of doing a bog-standard apple jelly I mixed in a combination of mint, rosemary and thyme.

Apple and herb jelly

INGREDIENTS

- 1 basin or basket of apples, windfalls are fine if not too damaged
- 1 bunch of fresh mint plus some extra very finely chopped
- 1 small bunch of fresh thyme
- 2–3 fresh rosemary sprigs
- jam sugar with added pectin

Remove any bruised parts or evidence of insect activity from the apples, then cut them up roughly, pips, skin and all. Tip into a preserving pan with a good bunch of fresh mint, a few sprigs of thyme and a couple of sprigs of rosemary, along with enough water to come halfway up the apples. Put some jam jars into a warm oven to sterilise (see page 5).

Bring the fruit to the boil, then reduce the heat and simmer gently until everything is really soft. Pass it through a muslin or jelly bag and, when cold enough, squeeze out as much of the juice as you can. Measure the juice and add the same amount of granulated sugar or, as I did, the suggested quantity of jam sugar with added pectin. Stir until the sugar is dissolved, then boil until the setting point is reached on a jam thermometer, or according to the instructions on the pack of jam sugar. Pour the jam carefully into your hot jars. Seal, label and store in a cool, dark cupboard.

NOTE

If you wish to add some fresh mint to the jelly, wait until it is almost set before stirring in some very finely chopped mint leaves. By waiting, the mint will remain suspended in the jelly as against rising to the top and sitting there in a clump.

top to bottom: *A wonderful harvest; ready to roll; raspberry vinegar and apple and mint jelly*

AUG 23RD *When I was sorting out the chickens the other day (the three original girls are still on egg strike), I saw that the sloes were fat and juicy. I know you should let a frost get at them before making sloe gin, but I thought it might not be necessary for a jelly. I picked a pound of sloes and the same of blackberries plus three ripe eating apples, mixing them together.*

Yet another gift from our fisherman friend: a box of mackerel he had caught that night a mile and a half off the Brighton coast. Mackerel begins to taint almost as soon as it is caught and (in an ideal world) the only way I will eat them is fresh out of the sea. Gutted and with the heads removed, he showed me how to fillet them so I could fry goujons for lunch.

above: *Fresh mackerel straight out of the sea*

Mackerel goujons

INGREDIENTS

2 spanking fresh mackerel, gutted and filleted
2–3 tbsp plain flour
salt and ground black pepper
1–2 eggs (depending on size of eggs)
2–3 tbsp Panko crumbs (Japanese breadcrumbs) or fresh brown or white breadcrumbs
2 tbsp–1 cup oil
1–2 lemon(s)

Check for any remaining bones, then dust the fillets of mackerel in flour seasoned with salt and pepper. Have two dishes ready, one with a beaten egg and the other with Panko crumbs. Dip the fish first in the egg, then in the breadcrumbs. In the meantime, heat the oil. Carefully place the crumbed fillets into the pan and shallow-fry for a minute or two, then turn them over a fry for another minute until crisp and golden. Serve with a tartare sauce and lemon wedges.

TIP

Use one hand for 'dry', the other for 'wet' when preparing the goujons.

Tartare sauce

INGREDIENTS

1 tbsp gherkins, chopped
1 tbsp capers, chopped
1 tbsp shallots, chopped
1 tbsp fresh parsley, chopped
2 tbsp good-quality mayonnaise

Mix all the ingredients together.

TIP

If you don't have gherkins or capers but have a green pepper, this is an excellent substitute.

AUG 24TH

This is a store cupboard necessity and, if you make it yourself, you know exactly what goes into it – no E numbers, no preservatives, just pure, unadulterated goodness. However, you will need two things: a large preserving pan and a lot of time but it's worth it. The following quantities are what Ma used for a family of five, but I halve and quarter them, which is a lot easier and more manageable.

above: *Sun-ripened goodness*
below: *Tomato ketchup*

Tomato ketchup

INGREDIENTS

3.6kg (8lb) ripe tomatoes
6 onions, chopped
2 large red peppers, deseeded and roughly chopped
2 large garlic cloves, crushed
either 1 red chilli or ½ tsp dried chilli flakes
2 bay leaves, torn
1 tbsp celery seeds (NOT celery salt)
1 tbsp mustard seeds
1 tsp black peppercorns
1 cinnamon stick, broken in 2–3 pieces
115g (4oz) soft brown sugar
115g (4oz) caster sugar
1 tbsp salt
2 cups red wine vinegar

Put your clean bottles or jars into a warm oven to sterilise (see page 5). Roughly chop the tomatoes and put them into the pan, pips, skin and everything. Add the onions to the pot with the peppers, garlic and enough water barely to cover the vegetables. Bring to the boil, then reduce the heat and simmer until they are completely soft, stirring now and again. Take off the heat and whizz with a hand-held blender. Don't worry if there are still some lumpy bits.

Put the spices into a muslin bag or a piece of muslin and secure it tightly. Add this to the tomato mix along with all the other ingredients. Bring to the boil and stir. Leave to cook on a gentle bubble for simply ages until the liquid has reduced by at least a half remembering that it will continue to thicken as it gets cold. When you are happy with the consistency, gradually pass it through a sieve to remove any pips, seeds, etc. Pour the mixture carefully into the hot bottles or jars and wait until it is cold before sealing. Store in the fridge. This can be eaten immediately and should last a couple of months at least if stored correctly. It really peps up a homemade burger.

above: *Coriander, my favourite herb*

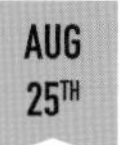

Last night's supper was a curry inspired yet again by my great-great grandmother. Curries improve with flavour if made the day before.

Chicken curry with red peppers and coconut milk

INGREDIENTS

- 2 tbsp sunflower oil
- 2 chicken breasts (skin on or off)
- 1 large onion, sliced
- 1 red pepper, deseeded and chopped
- 2–3 heaped tsp medium curry powder
- 2 fat garlic cloves, chopped
- 1 medium red or green chilli, deseeded and finely sliced
- 400ml (14fl oz) can reduced-fat coconut milk
- 400g (14oz) can chickpeas, rinsed and drained
- vegetable or chicken stock or water
- salt and ground black pepper
- a handful of fresh coriander, roughly chopped

Heat the oil in a large pan over a moderate heat and brown the chicken pieces on both sides for about 3 minutes. Remove from the pan and put to one side. Cook the sliced onion until it begins to soften and takes on a little colour. Add the red pepper and cook a further 2 minutes. Add the curry powder, garlic and chilli, stir for a minute, then add the chicken, coconut milk, chickpeas and enough stock or water so that the chicken is nearly covered with liquid. Season with salt and pepper, but go gently on the salt in case your stock has sufficient.

NOTE

Don't, whatever you do, taste at this point as the chicken is still raw in the middle and could give you a nasty tum. Wait until it is thoroughly cooked before adjusting the seasoning.

Stir gently and cook over a moderate heat for about 20 minutes, or until the chicken is cooked through and the sauce reduced and thickened. Stir in the coriander and cover. Keep warm while you cook some plain basmati rice and a vegetable. We had French beans from the garden.

I always like to make a cooling cucumber raita (see opposite).

Cucumber raita

Mix all the ingredients together.

TIP

Add a pinch of ground coriander and cumin if you want to lift it a touch.

INGREDIENTS

7.5–10cm (3–4in) piece cucumber, grated
2 tbsp natural yogurt
1 tbsp fresh mint, chopped
salt and ground black pepper

AUG 26TH

My tabbouleh

Cook the bulgur wheat according to the pack instructions, and when cold, add the vegetables and herbs, and stir to combine. Mix enough lemon juice, olive oil and seasoning together to make a dressing, then pour over the tabbouleh.

Scrumptious.

INGREDIENTS

100g (3½oz) bulgur wheat
½ cucumber, spiralised
1 green pepper, deseeded and finely chopped
1 red pepper, deseeded and finely chopped
several spring onions, finely sliced
3 tomatoes, finely chopped (if you wish, remove skins and pips but adding an extra one for more flavour)
2 tbsp fresh mint, chopped
2 tbsp fresh parsley, chopped
juice of 1 large lemon
olive oil to taste
salt and ground black pepper

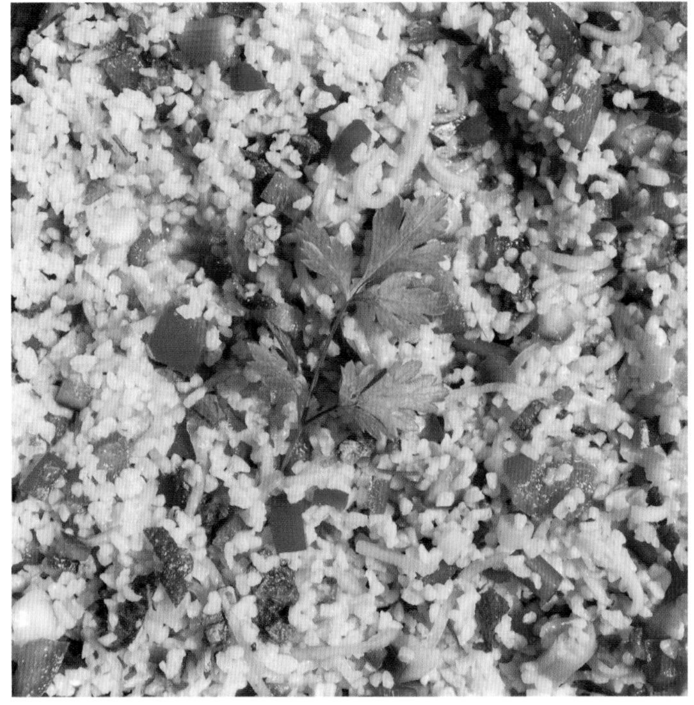

left: *My tabbouleh*

Yesterday, in between torrential rainstorms, I picked a bowl of raspberries and some blackberries to make flavoured vinegars filling pretty bottles I have saved for this purpose.

Raspberry and blackberry vinegars

INGREDIENTS

ripe raspberries
ripe blackberries
red/cider/or white wine vinegar

above: *A variety of flavoured vinegars*
below: *More vinegars and basil oil*

Divide the fruit between sterilised (see page 5), wide screwtop jars, then pour in enough of your choice of vinegar to cover the fruit. Place the jars on a sunny windowsill for a couple of weeks, giving a daily shake or two. Finally, strain through a muslin or fine cloth into a jug and fill re-sterilised bottles. Store for 3–6 months and use in salads, casseroles, gravy, etc.

Basil oil

INGREDIENTS

handfuls of fresh basil leaves
olive oil

In spite of a lack of sunshine recently, the herbs are still performing and I decided to make some basil oil. I picked a big bunch of leaves, rinsed them under the tap and shook off as much of the water as I could. I put them into a mini blender along with a small bottle (350ml/12fl oz) of olive oil and blitzed it. Then, I poured the mixture into a saucepan and brought it almost to the boil and let it heat gently for about 3 minutes before straining it into a jug through a small piece of muslin, and then into the sterilised (see page 5) bottle. This must be consumed within 10–12 days, so I put a sticky label on it with the 'use-by' date. It's very important to do this because sometimes bacteria can grow if it is kept too long, particularly if you put garlic into oil or vinegar.

Toasted halloumi and pine nut sunny summer salad

INGREDIENTS

enough halloumi for each person, sliced
a splash of sherry vinegar
1 tbsp olive oil
salt and ground black pepper
pine nuts, quickly toasted in a dry pan for 2 minutes
tomatoes, chopped (I was able to pick some Green Zebra tomatoes but any will do)
little gem lettuce, torn into pieces
1 red onion, sliced
cucumber, spiralised or finely chopped
fresh basil leaves

Slice the halloumi and fry gently in a fairly warm pan for 1 minute, then turn and fry for another minute, or until slightly brown. Make the dressing by mixing the vinegar, olive oil and seasoning together. Mix the halloumi with the rest of the salad ingredients and the dressing, then garnish with basil. Simple, clean and light.

above: *Halloumi and pine nut salad*
below: *The hut (now painted in traditional black) and rose arch in all its splendour*

AUG 27TH *As I have already mentioned the shepherd's hut is very high off the ground with two large and two smaller wheels. I decided to do a bit of Miss Marpling and googled Rustons of Lincoln, who made them. Up came several pictures of old farm equipment, such as threshers or engines to make the said threshers work, all with big wheels at the back, smaller ones at the front, so it is possible that our hut started life as one of these items of agricultural machinery.*

above: *Raised beds of chard, carrots, runner beans an gladioli for picking*

AUG 29TH *The hedges are spangled with autumn berries, hopefully not portents of a harsh winter to come.*

Another mixed vegetable stir-fry

INGREDIENTS

1 nest rice or egg noodles per person, dried or ready to use
1 tbsp vegetable oil
1 courgette, cut into small sticks (I'm giving the spiraliser a day off)
about ½ cucumber, chopped into small pieces
about ½–1 fennel bulb, finely sliced
3–4 spring onions, finely sliced
enough French beans for each person, sliced
1 green pepper, deseeded and finely chopped
2.5cm (1in) piece fresh root ginger, peeled and grated
1 red or green chilli, deseeded and chopped
soy sauce
toasted sesame oil (optional)

Cook the noodles according to the instructions on the packet. Heat the wok over a high heat, add the oil, then all the vegetables and stir frequently, adding a good splash of soy. When they are nearly cooked, add the noodles. Serve immediately, drizzled with a splash of sesame oil if you have some, once the noodles are heated through.

My brother Neil came to lunch and I made our favourite Catalan snack, a perfect, barbecue nibble.

Pan con tomate

INGREDIENTS

1 ciabatta, sourdough or French bread
garlic cloves to rub on to the bread
2–3 large beef tomatoes
olive oil
salt

TIP

To make a more substantial dish, small strips of anchovies can be laid on top, in which case don't sprinkle on any salt.

Toast some slices of bread of your choice and rub with garlic. Cut a large beef tomato in half and squidge this on to the bread. Drizzle with olive oil and sprinkle with salt. This can be done in advance. Eat and enjoy.

Years ago, Jimmy and I were invited to have supper with a friend at the Garrick. Our host's wife ordered gulls' eggs and celery salt, which at today's prices (retail, not restaurant), are at least £8 a pop. I love quail eggs served this way. Today however, I hard-boiled some of the hens' eggs as the girls have been extremely generous with their offerings.

Savoury eggs

INGREDIENTS

1–2 hard-boiled hens' eggs per person
1–2 tbsp good-quality mayonnaise
celery salt
ground black pepper
paprika
fresh chives, chopped and parsley

Cut the hard-boiled eggs in half and remove the yolks. Mix them with a little mayonnaise, celery salt and black pepper. Using a fluted nozzle, pipe the mixture back into the whites. Put them on to a dish and, using a tea strainer, dust a little paprika over them plus a sprinkle of chives and parsley.

below: *Jonathan Livingston, I presume?*

AUTUMN

above: *The crops keep on coming*

Spicy vegetable patties

INGREDIENTS

mixture of red, green and yellow peppers, de-seeded and finely chopped
1 large garlic clove, peeled and chopped
1 red onion, peeled and finely chopped
1 large green chilli, de-seeded and chopped
1 fresh sweetcorn cob, kernels cut off
1 courgette, finely chopped
1 egg
1 tbsp plain flour
½ tsp ground coriander
½ tsp ground turmeric
¼ tsp ground cumin
salt and ground black pepper
vegetable or sunflower oil to fry

Mix all the ingredients together except the oil, which you heat in a pan. Place a large tablespoonful of the mixture in the hot oil. Cook for 5 minutes, then turn over and cook a further 3 minutes. Serve hot with tomato ketchup or mango chutney.

Store cupboard sups

INGREDIENTS

Maille mayonnaise (this is quite the nicest commercial mayonnaise I have tasted)
1 salmon fillet
salt and ground black pepper
1 standard pouch of pre-cooked red and white quinoa
1 bunch of spring onions, trimmed and finely sliced
juice of ½ lemon
fresh coriander, chopped

Turn on the grill. Spread the mayonnaise on top of the salmon fillet, season with salt and pepper and place under the medium grill for 5 minutes. At the same time, warm the quinoa (still in its pouch) in a pan of boiling water. Empty the contents into a bowl and mix in the spring onions, lemon juice and chopped coriander. Place the grilled salmon on top plus another small spoonful of mayonnaise and a dash more lemon juice and serve.

Crunchy salad with mozzarella

INGREDIENTS

cooked beetroot, sliced
tomato, sliced
cucumber, chopped
radishes, sliced
sunflower and pumpkin seeds
light mozzarella, torn
olive oil to drizzle
balsamic vinegar to drizzle
salt and ground black pepper.

Layer all the ingredients in a bowl and season to taste. I also added a clipping or two of pea shoots and micro rocket shoots (three weeks ago I took Monty D's advice and sowed these in seed trays in the greenhouse).

above: *Crunchy salad with mozzarella*
below: *The family who dines together, stays together*

SEPT 3RD

Neil gave me a load of Conference pears. I had already picked a basin of raspberries and there were dozens of apples, which Jimmy had gathered, so I decided to combine them into a jelly.

Apple, pear and raspberry jelly

A MIX OF:

- apples
- pears
- raspberries
- jam sugar with pectin
- a knob of butter (about 1 heaped tsp)

I roughly chopped the apples and pears, including the pips and skin and put them in a preserving pan with the raspberries and enough water to go halfway up the fruit. I brought it gently to the boil and then reduced the heat and simmered it until the fruit was soft and could be squashed with a potato masher. I poured it into a large piece of muslin placed in a sieve and strained it over a bowl until cool enough to squeeze out the last of the juice. I measured the juice and put it into the now-clean preserving pan on to heat and added an equal amount of jam sugar, stirring until it dissolved, plus a knob of butter, skimming off any foam, which may form. Once a good rolling boil was achieved I let it cook for about 4 minutes and then poured it into clean, hot, sterilised jars (see page 5). The colour was fabulous: clear and jewel-like and tasted like heaven – a really good alternative to redcurrant jelly.

above: *Soft autumn sunlight*
right: *Harvest time*

Concentrated roasted tomatoes and red peppers

above: *A last hurrah*
below: *Fruit alcohols for Christmas*

INGREDIENTS

assortment of tomatoes, large ones cut in half
2 onions, peeled and sliced
2 celery sticks, chopped
2 red peppers, deseeded and roughly chopped or torn into pieces
any herbs you have to hand, such as basil, thyme, marjoram or parsley
1 tsp granulated sugar
½ cup olive oil
salt and ground black pepper

Preheat the oven to 200°C (180°C fan) mark 6. Throw all the vegetables and herbs into a roasting dish, sprinkle with the sugar (this counteracts the acidity in the tomatoes), pour on the olive oil and season. Roast in the oven until there are signs that the tomato skins are beginning to singe. Leave to cool, then pass through a sieve. Pour into small dishes or bags and, once cold, put in the freezer. It can be frozen for up to three months and used as a base for soup with the addition of vegetable or chicken stock, or as a pasta sauce.

I picked a load of very ripe strawberries yesterday and instead of turning them into jam or using them to flavour vinegar I experimented with gin.

Strawberry liqueur

INGREDIENTS

strawberries, hulled and quartered
granulated sugar
alcohol of your choice, such as whisky, gin, vodka

TIP

Raspberries and blackberries make an excellent alternative.

Quarter fill a sterilised bottle (see page 5) with sugar, then using a funnel and the handle of a wooden spoon, push the strawberries into the bottle up to the top. Pour in the alcohol, seal securely and shake to mix with the sugar and fruit. Macerate for the next couple of months and it will be ready for Christmas, remembering to give it a shake every now and again until all the sugar had dissolved.

Savoury tomato baked custard

INGREDIENTS

- enough cherry tomatoes (kept whole) and/or other tomatoes, thickly sliced to coat the bottom of the dish
- fresh herbs, such as oregano, basil or thyme, chopped or torn if using basil
- 4 eggs
- 1 tbsp plain flour
- ½ tub crème fraîche
- 1 tbsp milk
- salt and ground black pepper
- about 85g (3oz) cheese, grated (it's up to you what sort you use. I mix up bits and bobs leftover in the fridge)
- dried brown breadcrumbs, if you like

above: *Fresh herbs at the kitchen door*
below: *Savoury tomato baked custard*

Preheat the oven to 200°C (180°C fan) mark 6. Lay the tomatoes in the bottom of a flan dish or shallow baking dish and sprinkle over the herbs. In a bowl, beat the eggs into the flour, removing any lumps, then add the crème fraîche, milk, salt and pepper. Fold in the grated cheese, then pour the custard over the tomatoes. Strew with a few extra herbs.

I happened to have baked some stale brown bread and turned it into crumbs so I scattered 1–2 tbsp on top to give it a bit of crunch. Bake in the oven for about 20 minutes, or until it is fluffed up, firm and golden brown. Allow to cool slightly before tucking in. This can be a light lunch accompanied with a green salad, or to go with a roast chicken, beef or lamb.

SEPT 5TH

We have unwelcome guests: rats. They are everywhere and are as bold as brass, bristling their whiskers and sitting on their hunkers, refusing to scamper off when we try to frighten them away. Where is the Pied Piper when you need him? Time to call in Mr Pest Controller.

Because of our English climate I have more success when growing peppers and aubergines in the safe confines of the greenhouse. This soup is packed full of flavour and goodness.

Roasted red pepper soup

INGREDIENTS

- 4 large red peppers, deseeded and roughly chopped or torn into pieces
- 2 onions, peeled and sliced
- 2–3 garlic cloves, peeled and chopped
- 2 carrots, peeled and sliced
- 1 celery stick, sliced
- 2–3 tbsp olive oil
- a scattering of dried mixed Italian herbs
- a sprinkle of dried chilli flakes or 1 red chilli, chopped (dried flakes are hotter because they include the seeds)
- salt and ground black pepper
- 400g (14oz) can chopped tomatoes
- ½ tsp granulated sugar
- 2½ cups good chicken stock (fresh, cube or jelly pot)
- fresh basil leaves to garnish

above: *Rattus rattus, or should it be ratti ratti?*
below: *A colourful cornucopia*

Preheat the oven to 200°C (180°C fan) mark 6. Place the vegetables into a roasting tray, drizzle with the olive oil and scatter over the dried herbs and chilli. Season well. Roast in the oven for 30 minutes, or until the vegetables are starting to singe. Transfer the mixture to a saucepan and add the tomatoes, sugar and chicken stock. Bring to the boil, then blitz in a blender or with a hand-held blender. Check on the seasoning before serving with a few fresh basil leaves torn on top.

With gardening you win some, you lose some. This year I have been able to grow the most wonderful carrots with not a hint of carrot fly, hardly any splitting or dividing and sweet as a nut.

Beetroot slaw

INGREDIENTS

raw beetroot, peeled and grated or spiralised
cucumber, sliced or spiralised
fennel bulb, finely sliced
1 celery stick, finely chopped
spring onions, sliced
raw young kohlrabi, either grated or finely chopped
carrot, spiralised or grated
radishes, finely sliced

Mix all the vegetables with a light dressing made from:
good-quality mayonnaise
plain yogurt
balsamic vinegar
lemon juice

There was plenty leftover for tomorrow perhaps served with sardines on fried bread.

SEPT 12TH

Where did the 'summer' go? The beautiful weather in April and May heralded, or so we thought, a year to remember but we were hoodwinked. The winds over the last two days have brought down apples, branches and leaves and the lawn is littered with debris. How sad it is to see the major part of the year well behind us and the prospect of a harsh winter to come. However, there are delights in store: the smell of bonfires, exhausted, damp but happy dogs lying in front of an open hearth in a country pub, the crackle of leaves under foot and sun on frosted seed heads.

above: *Beetroot slaw*
below: *Autumn has arrived*

SEPT 13TH

News from the pickle factory: the continuing gales have brought down so many apples that I couldn't put off making chutney any longer. Also, until now, the tomato crop has been abysmal, but once I started picking I soon filled my apron with ripe fruit.

above: *Apples and tomatoes ready for business*

Tomato and apple chutney

INGREDIENTS

- equal quantities of apples, onions and tomatoes
- for 450g (1lb) each of onions/tomatoes/apples use 2½ cups (plus a little extra) vinegar and about 400g (14oz) sugar (I used a mixture of demerara and muscovado sugar)
- 1 tsp salt for every 450g (1lb) vegetables
- 1 cup sultanas to 450g (1lb) apples

FOR THE MIXED SPICES

- 1 cinnamon stick, broken into pieces
- ½ tsp celery salt
- 1 tsp whole allspice
- 1 tsp ground ginger or 2.5cm (1in) piece fresh root ginger, peeled and grated
- as many dried chillies as you dare (I don't like it too hot and added ⅓ tsp)

Secure all the spices in a square of muslin, which you remove when the chutney is cooked.

Peel, core and roughly chop the apples and keep to one side. Peel and finely slice the onions and put into a large saucepan with the vinegar and bag of spices. Bring gently to the boil, then reduce the heat and simmer for about 30 minutes until nearly soft. Add the tomatoes and apples and cook gently for 10 minutes, stirring every now and then. Next, add the sugar and salt, stirring until dissolved, then add the sultanas. Allow the chutney to cook on a gentle bubble, stirring to prevent it from sticking or burning, until it is a thick consistency. Pour into hot sterilised jars (see page 5) using a funnel, then seal, label and store in a cool cupboard for at least three months allowing it to mature. If you do it now, it will be ready for Christmas.

SEPT 14TH

I am always looking for economical but tasty ways to cook a main meal and have enjoyed pigs' cheeks many a time in Spain when on holiday in Catalunya. Think belly of pork, lamb neck chops or breast - pigs' cheeks are not offal. They are very low in fat and if cooked the following way will give you the most tender, sweet mouthfuls you could imagine. I did stage 1 the day before and then stage 2 the next day, the flavours improving overnight.

Braised pigs' cheeks

INGREDIENTS

1 packet of fresh pigs' cheeks (available from good supermarkets)
olive oil
1 onion, very finely chopped
1 celery stick, finely chopped
1 carrot, very finely chopped
½ tsp dried mixed herbs
1 fat clove garlic, crushed
a splash of good red wine (Rioja is ideal – a large wine glassful – you can drink the rest with the dish)
salt and ground black pepper

STAGE 1

Preheat the oven to 150°C (130°C fan) mark 2. Rinse the pigs' cheeks under cold water and pat dry. Heat a smidgen of olive oil in a flameproof casserole and carefully add the pigs' cheeks. Fry for 2 minutes on each side to seal, then remove from the pan and keep to one side. Put the onion, celery and carrot into the same pan and cook for about 5 minutes, stirring all the while. Add the meat and any juices, then the herbs and crushed garlic. Stir and add the wine then season well. Bring gently to the boil, cover with a lid and put into the oven to simmer for about 1½ hours.

Remove from the oven and prod the meat. It should be very soft and tender. Allow to cool, then put in the fridge until the next day.

STAGE 2

About an hour before you are going to eat this dish, preheat the oven to 200°C (180°C fan) mark 6 and transfer the meat and juices to a shallow ovenproof dish. Place the dish on the middle shelf of the oven and cook for about 15–20 minutes, basting the meat with the juices during reheating. Serve piping hot with chips and no extra vegetables, Spanish style. I am a cheat and use frozen oven-cook French fries.

TIP

To cut down on the cooking time you could try using sliced pork tenderloin, but braise the vegetables first before adding the meat.

above: *My watercolour of happy piggies*
below: *Braised pigs' cheeks*

Lime and ginger chicken

INGREDIENTS

1 tbsp soy sauce
1 small red chilli, deseeded and finely chopped
1 fat clove garlic, chopped
juice of 1 lime
about 2cm (¾in) piece fresh root ginger, peeled and grated
1 chicken breast on the bone (or leg and thigh if you prefer)
2 tsp vegetable or sunflower oil
1 small glass of white wine, plus a splash of water
salt and ground black pepper
fresh coriander

In a bowl, mix the soy, chilli, garlic, lime juice and ginger together, then add the chicken, rubbing the juices into all the nooks and crannies. Either put everything into a plastic bag and seal well, or cover the bowl with clingfilm. Leave in the fridge for at least an hour.

Preheat the oven to 200°C (180°C fan) mark 6. Heat the oil in a flameproof casserole and gently brown the chicken on both sides. Add the wine, a splash of water and season well with pepper, but go easy on the salt as the soy may be sufficient. Put the lid on the casserole and cook in the oven for about 20 minutes, or until the juices run clear making sure the liquid hasn't all evaporated. If so, add a little more water or wine. When ready to serve, chop some fresh coriander leaves and scatter over the chicken. I usually serve with plain basmati rice and a vegetable and mango chutney (see page 119).

TIP

Instead of buying expensive packs of chicken breasts it is far cheaper to buy a whole bird and cut it up into pieces, freezing what you don't need for another day.

above: *Garlic neatly plaited*

above: *Chilli kebabs drying in the sun*

This is a lovely, light, vegetarian dish and the following will be plenty for two.

Spicy mushroom stir fry mix

INGREDIENTS

- a little sunflower or vegetable oil
- 1 medium red onion, finely sliced
- 1–2 garlic cloves, chopped
- ½ tsp ground coriander
- ½ tsp ground cumin
- ½ tsp ground turmeric
- 1 small red chilli or ½ larger one, deseeded and finely chopped
- 2cm (¾in) piece fresh root ginger, peeled and grated
- 2–3 large flat, field mushrooms, peeled and sliced (these remain nice and 'meaty')
- 2 large tomatoes, roughly chopped
- 400g (14oz) can chickpeas, rinsed and drained (I cooked a handful of fresh borlotti beans instead and they were lovely and creamy in texture)
- 1 small bag baby spinach leaves
- fresh coriander leaves, chopped
- salt and ground black pepper

Heat the wok over a high heat, add a splash of oil, then add the onion and stir-fry for a couple of minutes until just beginning to soften, but not brown. Add the garlic, spices, chilli and ginger and stir quickly for about a minute. Add the mushrooms, tomatoes, chickpeas and a little water to moisten. Stir, cover and simmer gently for about 5 minutes. Add the spinach, stir, cover and cook for a further 5 minutes. Throw in a good handful of chopped coriander, season and serve immediately with plain boiled rice, chutney and any other side dishes such as cucumber raita (see page 91), naan bread, etc.

SEPT 16TH *Bed socks and hot water bottles have emerged from their summer quarters and melancholy prevails as I watch the swallows gather and settle on the television aerial, their bags packed and ready to leave for South Africa. April seems an age away until they return.*

This miserable weather has made me yearn for something hot and comforting.

Vegetable curry

In a hot pan with the oil, fry the aubergine and onions until soft. Add the ginger, garlic, spices and chilli and continue frying for a couple of minutes, stirring gently. Add the squash, tomatoes, spinach, red lentils and stock and cook until the lentils are soft. The lentils will absorb a lot of liquid so you may have to add extra stock or water. When the lentils are cooked, season with salt and pepper, sprinkle with fresh coriander leaves and serve with perfumed basmati rice.

Curry to me is not about heat but about flavour and the spices used; this turned out to be one of the nicest I have eaten.

INGREDIENTS

2 tbsp vegetable or sunflower oil
1 large aubergine, sliced
2 onions, sliced
2.5cm (1in) piece fresh root ginger, peeled and grated
2 garlic cloves, crushed
½ tsp ground turmeric
½ tsp ground coriander
½ tsp ground cumin
½ tsp garam masala
1 red chilli, chopped (keep the seeds if you want extra oomph)
1 pattypan squash or ½ butternut squash, peeled and cut into pieces (if using butternut remove the seeds when cutting the squash into pieces)
3 tomatoes, chopped
1 small bag of spinach
1 cup red lentils
2½ cups chicken or vegetable stock
salt and ground black pepper
fresh coriander leaves

left: *Vegetable curry*

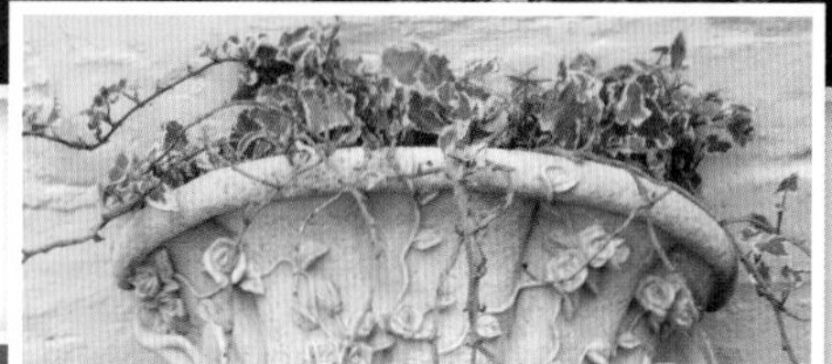

SEPT 18TH

Baked sea bass and potatoes

INGREDIENTS

3 medium potatoes, sliced
1 fennel bulb, finely sliced (keep some of the green fronds for stuffing the fish)
2 garlic cloves, sliced
a good slug of olive oil
½ tsp dried marjoram
salt and ground black pepper
1 good-sized and really fresh sea bass
a handful of cherry tomatoes
1 cup white wine
1 lemon, cut into quarters

Preheat the oven to 200°C (180°C fan) mark 6. I laid the vegetables on the bottom of a baking dish, drizzled in the olive oil, sprinkled over the marjoram and seasoned lightly. Covered loosely with foil I baked it in the oven for about 30 minutes, or until the potatoes were almost cooked.

Before I added the fish, I made sure the scales were removed by scraping along the skin with a knife and then rinsed well. I filled the cavity with the reserved fennel fronds, scored the skin with a sharp knife and placed it on top of the vegetables, added a handful of cherry tomatoes, a further drizzle of olive oil and the dry white wine, plus more seasoning. I put it back into the oven and baked it, uncovered for 15–20 minutes, then served it with lemon wedges.

below: *Baked sea bass and potatoes*

SEPT 19TH

The apple tree has never looked more beautiful. It is as though a scene from Snow White has sprung to life, as the fruit are so very red and shiny. It's as though each one had been polished with a silk cloth. Sadly, they don't store and some are already turning too soft to use, so it's a rush against time to secure as many for the freezer for winter puddings and to make into jelly or chutney.

top: *Raw French apple tart*
bottom: *Cooked French apple tart*

French apple tart

INGREDIENTS

250g (9oz) plain flour
1 egg yolk
150g (5oz) soft, slightly salted butter (or unsalted, plus a pinch of salt)
5–6 eating apples
juice of ½ lemon
50g (1¾oz) ground almonds
50g (1¾oz) demerara or light brown sugar
1 tsp ground cinnamon
30g (1oz) melted butter

Sift the flour into a bowl and make a well in the centre. Add the egg yolk and butter and rub together very lightly with your fingertips. When it resembles breadcrumbs add 5 tbsp cold water, little by little, mixing it in with two knives. You may not need all the water to bind it together but also, you may need a drop or two more. Do not knead but gather together into a ball, then wrap in clingfilm before chilling it in the fridge for an hour.

In the meantime, peel and finely slice the apples and place into a bowl of cold water with the lemon juice – this will stop them turning brown. Mix together the almonds, sugar and cinnamon.

Preheat the oven to 200°C (180°C fan) mark 6. Remove the pastry from the fridge and roll out to fit a 10 inch buttered flan ring or loose-based tart tin. Trim the edges and prick the bottom with a fork. Sprinkle the base with half the almond mixture and arrange the apple slices on top in a neat pattern. Brush the melted butter over the apples before sprinkling over the other half of the almond mix. Bake for about 30 minutes, or until the pastry is cooked through. Serve with whipped double cream or crème fraîche.

SEPT 21ST *To coincide with the colour scheme of the interior of the hut, which is going to be a flat, chalky white we now have a new member of the family: an albino pheasant. He/she (sex currently undecided) appeared a week ago and is very underweight probably due to the fact that its beak was severely deformed. Neil managed to corner it by the barn enabling me to trim away the damaged part of the beak with some nail clippers. It was a painless exercise, like cutting fingernails and it set upon some of the chickens' corn with gusto, followed by a drink. It has since become quite tame and has taken to sleeping in the greenhouse, eating happily from our hands. I hope the fox doesn't make a nocturnal appearance.*

above: *Chalky*
below: *Tomato pastry slice*

Tomato pastry slice

INGREDIENTS

1 pack of ready-rolled all butter puff pastry
1 small tub or ½ large tub cream cheese, enough to spread over the pastry
1 red onion, thinly sliced into rings
4 tomatoes, sliced
1 tsp dried Italian herbs
1 garlic clove, chopped
salt and ground black pepper
olive oil to drizzle

Preheat the oven to 200°C (180°C fan) mark 6. Lay a rectangle of pastry on to a very lightly greased baking tray and prick with a fork. Spread on a good thick layer of cream cheese, then scatter the onion and tomatoes on top, sprinkle with the herbs, add the garlic, season and drizzle with a little olive oil. Bake in the centre of the oven until the pastry is cooked through. Serve warm or at room temperature with a green salad.

SEPT 23RD

Goat's cheese and chard quiche

INGREDIENTS

1 standard pack of ready-rolled all butter puff pastry
1 bunch of Swiss chard leaves
1 red onion, sliced
1 tbsp olive oil
goat's cheese of your choice (I chose a small barrel shape), broken into pieces
1 tbsp fresh parsley, chopped
few fresh thyme sprigs, leaves pulled off stalks
2–3 eggs
150ml (¼ pint) single or double cream
salt and ground black pepper

Line a greased 10 inch flan ring or loose-based tart tin with the pastry and trim off the excess. Prick the base with a fork, lay on a piece of baking parchment, fill with ceramic beads, rice grains or dried pulses and bake in the oven for about 10 minutes. Remove the parchment and beans and bake for a further 3 minutes.

In the meantime, prepare the chard. Trim the stalk end and fold the leaves into a saucepan. Don't cut the leaves when raw as the stalks will oxidise and go black. This doesn't affect the flavour but it isn't so attractive. Add a little boiling water, push down and stir the leaves during cooking, which takes about 5–6 minutes. Drain thoroughly and roughly chop. You can always cut off the stalks and just use the leafy parts, using the stalks later, simply steam and serve with butter and lemon juice, rather like asparagus – perhaps with a little chopped parsley.

In a frying pan, soften the onion in the olive oil, then add to the chard and lay on the pastry case. Dot the pieces of cheese over the chard and sprinkle with the herbs. Beat the eggs with the cream, season well and pour over the quiche. Bake in the oven for 30–40 minutes until fully cooked, browned and puffed up.

top: *Goat's cheese and chard quiche*
bottom: *Sisters, such devoted sisters...*

This is a very gentle and healthy way to eat fish.

Easy salmon

INGREDIENTS

2 or 3 shakes of soy sauce
2.5cm (1in) piece fresh root ginger, peeled and sliced
1–2 garlic cloves, crushed
1 red chilli, deseeded and finely chopped or a pinch of dried chilli flakes (these are hotter than fresh because they include the seeds)
juice of 1 lemon
1 salmon fillet per person (I prefer the flat, triangular tail pieces rather than wedges)
3–4 spring onions, sliced

Mix the soy, ginger, garlic, chilli and lemon juice together in a non-metallic container, add the salmon, turning it once or twice until it is well covered in the marinade and place in the fridge for an hour or so if possible.

Place the fish and marinade into a small bowl or shallow dish which will fit inside a steamer – or one which will sit on a trivet in a wok. Sprinkle over the sliced spring onions, put the lid on the steamer or wok and cook for about 8 minutes. When cooked lift off the fish and remove the skin, discarding the cooking vegetables and marinade juices. Serve with new potatoes or noodles tossed in a little soy sauce.

below: *The hut finally in position*

SEPT 25TH

Yesterday, after enormous care the shepherd's hut was towed to its resting place in the field. It was shrouded in mist this morning when I went to check that it had survived the night and with the warm, autumnal sunshine filtering through it restored my soul.

SEPT 26TH

Autumn salad

INGREDIENTS

1 chicory head, sliced
1 pack of mixed radishes, sliced
1 red onion, sliced
1 standard bag or 1 bunch of watercress
6 walnuts, broken into pieces (new season's if you can find them)
several slices Parma ham, torn into pieces
1 tbsp sunflower oil
2 tsp red wine vinegar
juice of ½ lemon
salt and ground black pepper
½ cup grated Cheddar

Mix everything apart from the cheese together in a serving bowl. Sprinkle the cheese on top before serving.

TIP

If you have a bottle of walnut oil, use a little less of the sunflower and add 1 tsp of this. It really brings out the flavour – it enhances the slight bitterness of the chicory and the walnuts.

above: *Hollyhock, a cottage garden favourite*
left: *Autumn salad*

above: *The forest floor*

If mushroom soup is on the menu, rarely do I choose it because I'm not too keen on the earthy, musty flavour of the forest floor, but this recipe fits the bill.

Not too mushroomy soup

INGREDIENTS

2 tsp oil
1 shallot, finely chopped
1 small carrot, finely chopped
2 small celery sticks, or 1 large stick, finely sliced
225g (8oz) chestnut mushrooms, peeled and finely sliced
1 garlic clove, chopped
2½ cups good strong chicken stock
about 150ml (¼ pint) milk
salt and ground black pepper
fresh parsley, chopped

TIP

Tarragon goes really well with mushrooms and you can add a few leaves (about 2 tsp once chopped) towards the end of cooking.

Heat the oil in a saucepan and throw in the shallot, carrot and celery. Sweat the vegetables for about 5 minutes over a moderate heat, stirring every now and again. Add the mushrooms and garlic, stir, then add the liquid. If using a stock cube, you must taste the soup before adding any extra seasoning. Bring to the boil and simmer gently until the vegetables are cooked through. Remove from the heat and blitz with a hand-held blender, leaving it on the chunky side rather than smooth. Add the milk and blitz again. Check on the seasoning and serve sprinkled with chopped parsley. You can always stir in a little cream or crème fraîche just before serving.

SEPT 28TH

At last, after waiting with such anticipation, we have had the first honey from the hives in the bottom field. Our little guests have produced the most delicious thick, creamy, sweet treat and I cannot believe that it was made within eyesight of the kitchen window.

SEPT 29TH

This morning I did a big clear out of the fridge and fruit basket and found an overripe mango and two equally fruity pears too good to chuck on to the compost heap. Jimmy had also presented me with a selection of apples. Chutney it is.

Mixed fruit chutney

Put all the ingredients, except the sugar, into a preserving or stainless steel pan and bring to the boil. Reduce the heat and simmer until soft and much of the liquid has evaporated, stirring every now and again to prevent sticking and burning.

In the meantime, put four or so jam jars into the oven to warm and to sterilise (see page 5). When the fruit is soft, add the sugar and stir until it is dissolved. Bring to the boil and cook rapidly (with the protection of an anti-splatter thingy if you have one) until it is thick, dark and divides when you draw a wooden spoon across the bottom of the pan. This can take 30 minutes. Pour into the hot jars, seal and label. Keep in a dark, cool place for a month before enjoying.

INGREDIENTS

- 2 ripe pears, peeled and chopped
- 1 overripe mango, peeled and chopped
- 3 medium cooking apples, peeled and chopped
- 3 medium onions, chopped
- 2.5cm (1in) piece fresh root ginger, peeled and grated
- a handful of sultanas or raisins
- 1 heaped tsp salt
- 1½ cups red wine vinegar or cider or white wine vinegar
- 1 scant (under a level) tsp ground cinnamon
- 1 scant tsp ground cumin
- 1 scant tsp cayenne pepper
- 1 scant tsp ground coriander
- 1 large garlic clove, crushed
- 2½ cups demerara sugar

left: *Necessity is the mother of invention*

Comforting beef and mushroom stew

INGREDIENTS

- 1 tbsp oil
- 1 large slice well marbled stewing steak (about 450g/ 1lb), trimmed of gristle and fat and cut into 2.5cm (1in) chunks
- 1 large onion, finely sliced
- 3 large field mushrooms (more flavour than button), peeled and sliced
- 1–2 garlic cloves, finely chopped
- 1 tbsp concentrated tomato purée
- 150ml (¼ pint) red wine
- salt and ground black pepper

Preheat the oven to 200°C (180°C fan) mark 6. Begin by putting a small amount of oil in a flameproof casserole, and when hot (not smoking), gently brown the meat in small batches, turning it now and then until it is sealed and taking on a bit of colour. Remove the meat with a slotted spoon and put to one side.

Next, add the onion to the pan, stir and sweat over a moderate heat until it is starting to soften, about 5 minutes. Return the meat plus any juices to the pan and add the mushrooms, garlic and tomato purée. Pour in the red wine, season and stir. There must be enough wine for everything to cook in but it doesn't need to be covered with the liquid.

Bring slowly to the boil, cover and put into the oven to simmer for at least 1½ hours. Check every now and then to make sure it's not drying out. If so, add a little water.

I like to cook this a day in advance so that when the stew is quite cold I can remove any fat from the surface, also the flavours will develop overnight. Serve with creamy mashed potatoes, sweet potatoes or celeriac – even pasta – and something green.

below: *It looks like rain*

Prawn and egg salad

INGREDIENTS

- 1–2 standard packs ready-cooked cold water North Atlantic prawns
- 1 hard-boiled egg per person plus 1 extra, halved
- several fresh parsley sprigs, finely chopped
- paprika
- 1 large lettuce or 2 little gems
- rocket leaves
- shop-bought garlic bread
- 1 tbsp good-quality mayonnaise

Surround the prawns with the hard-boiled eggs, sprinkle with parsley and dust with paprika passed through a tea strainer. Make a green salad with the lettuce and rocket. Serve with hot garlic bread and a pot of mayonnaise.

This made a light, tasty and meal perfect for the exceptional and unseasonal midday heat.

Creamy topped raspberries

INGREDIENTS

1 standard punnet of raspberries
1 standard punnet of strawberries, hulled and cut in half
½ tub crème fraîche
equal amount of Greek yogurt
4 tsp dark muscovado sugar

Put the fruit into a glass bowl. Whip the crème fraîche with the yogurt, then spoon over the fruit and sprinkle with the muscovado sugar. Cover with clingfilm and leave in the fridge until needed and the sugar has dissolved.

top: *Ruby red raspberries*
bottom: *Houseboat at Shoreham*

A trip into the village resulted in bringing home lunch on special offer: some wonderfully fresh fish, straight out of the sea at Newhaven, which needs no fancy cooking.

Simple lemon sole

INGREDIENTS

1 small lemon sole or plaice per person, either left whole of filleted
plain flour, to coat
about 2 tbsp vegetable or sunflower oil
butter
juice of ½ lemon
salt and ground black pepper
a little fresh parsley, chopped

Dip the fish or fillets in flour to coat. Heat the oil in a frying pan and carefully lay the fish, skin-side down. After a minute or two, flip them over with a fish slice and cook a further 2 minutes, adding a good-sized knob of butter. This is for flavour – don't add it with the oil at the beginning. Add the lemon juice and season. Sprinkle with some chopped parsley and serve piping hot with crusty French bread and butter.

OCT 1ST *Today we start work on the wildflower meadow, which will become a paradise for the bees, their hives safely tucked away near the hedge, the water meadow and the stream. Wild flowers thrive on poor soil and so we have hired a digger to scoop off a layer of the rich green sand, cutting a curved swathe through the original grasses to add interest. Once the turf has been removed, the area will be scarified in preparation for sowing the flower mix, which was selected specially to suit our conditions. As soon as I can I intend to plant camassias and daffodils, although the latter should have been in the ground by the end of September. Tulips can wait to be planted quite happily until December – too soon and the bulbs can rot. I shall also plant the discarded bulbs from last year's tubs plus dozens of unused, out-of-date packets of flower seeds in the hope that some will germinate. Foxgloves, teasels, evening primroses and fluffy-leaved, statuesque yellow verbascum will self-seed themselves into the bargain.*

OCT 2ND *The weather today has been diluvian: torrential rain, wind and cold. In spite of this, I released the chickens who hate this weather, to have free run of the field letting them scratch about, anything to keep them occupied and happy. After a couple of hours, they had enough and gathered in a mournful huddle under the walnut tree grown from a nut by Ma. Singing the* Match of the Day *theme tune (don't ask) they followed me back to their run where, in spite of the inclement elements, the darlings produced four beautiful eggs.*

below: *The flooded water meadow*

OCT 4TH

I only enjoy a banana when it is bordering on green and inevitably end up with several uneaten and overripe ones. I hate waste and bake them with rum, orange juice and a little brown sugar, and served with double cream or crème fraîche. Alternatively, I make this 'bread'.

Easy peasy banana bread

INGREDIENTS

- 55g (2oz) soft butter (or unsalted, plus a pinch of salt)
- 150g (5oz) sugar (I used caster but you can use half demerara)
- 2 eggs, lightly beaten
- 225g (8oz) self-raising flour, sifted
- ½ tsp mixed spice
- finely grated zest of 1 orange
- a pinch of salt
- 2 ripe bananas, peeled and mashed

Preheat the oven to 200°C (180°C fan) mark 6. Butter a standard (450g/ 1lb) loaf tin. Cream the butter and sugar together in a bowl until light and fluffy. Mix in the beaten eggs, then fold in the flour, mixed spice, orange zest, salt and mashed bananas. Pour the mixture into the loaf tin and bake in the oven until the top is golden and cracks appear in the crust. Do the skewer test to see if it is cooked (an inserted skewer comes out clean). Mine took about 35 minutes but I have to confess there were some slightly burned bits. This didn't affect the moist texture inside; thank goodness.

Remove from the oven and wait a few minutes before taking it out of the tin. Cool on a wire rack and eat sliced with some butter. The addition of a few sultanas and currants, candied peel plus a pinch of ground ginger, cinnamon and mixed spice raises the bar.

right: *Easy peasy banana bread*

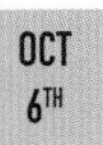

OCT 6TH

The season is now up and running for eating wild game, but only the brave will attempt to eat Squirrel Nutkin's cousin.

Pan-fried breasts of pheasant in apple sauce

INGREDIENTS

1 tbsp oil
1 shallot, finely chopped.
4 pheasant breasts, skin off
15g (½oz) butter
2–3 small sweet eating apples (Russets are my preferred choice). peeled and sliced
about 2 tbsp Calvados (apple brandy)
150ml (¼ pint) chicken stock
150ml (¼ pint) single cream
salt and ground black pepper
fresh parsley, chopped
a little oil

Heat a shallow frying pan and add the oil. When hot, add the chopped shallot and cook over a moderate heat, stirring every now and then, for 5 minutes, or until soft. Add the pheasant breasts and cook these gently for about 2 minutes. Turn them over, stir in the butter and the apples and simmer gently for a further 5 minutes, turning the breasts again. When the apple is nearly cooked, add a splash of Calvados and the chicken stock and bring gently to a bubbling boil. Pour in the cream and season with salt and pepper, stir and heat through. When ready to serve, sprinkle the top with some chopped parsley.

Boil some fluffy potatoes, then mash them with a little milk and butter and lots of salt and pepper and serve alongside something colourful like spring greens or braised red cabbage.

above: *The one that got away*

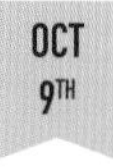

Carrot and coriander 'souper' soup

INGREDIENTS

1 bunch of carrots, chopped
1 large potato, peeled and chopped
a large handful of fresh coriander, stalks and all, roughly chopped, plus extra to sprinkle
2 garlic cloves, chopped
1 celery stick, chopped
juice of 1 large orange
stock cube (vegetable or chicken)
1¼ cups milk

Bung everything together, except the milk, in a large saucepan and add 2½ cups water. Bring to the boil, then reduce the heat and simmer. Don't overcook. Add the milk and blitz in a blender or use a hand-held blender. Sprinkle with more coriander leaves.

below: *Carrot and coriander 'souper' soup*

OCT 10TH

Shhhhhh... beef skirt – the chef's best kept secret

INGREDIENTS
piece of beef skirt
umami paste
olive oil
1 garlic clove, crushed

Skirt is situated beneath the ribs and is a fat free slab of beef generally used in slow cooked recipes but, if grilled or fried in a hot griddle pan, it is tender and has (in my mind) far more flavour than fillet. A friend brought over a piece for me to try, which he had marinated in umami paste and a little olive oil and garlic. It took no time at all to cook (keep it rare) and, once rested, I sliced it thinly across the grain. We ate it with fresh salad and baked potato wedges. It's terrific value and brilliant cooked on the barbecue.

Beef skirt is either very quickly cooked, i.e. grilled, fried or on a barbecue or simmered for a longer period in a casserole or stew. Generally, I brush each side of the steak with a little oil and cook it in a pre-heated cast iron griddle pan, seasoning it with salt and pepper. Alternatively, I infuse it briefly (10 minutes should be fine) in a marinade (see page 208).

OCT 11TH

The hut is up and running and open for business. After a very successful trip to the boot fair at the end of our lane on Sunday I was able to purchase a few last-minute items to complete the interior. I am so happy with the way it has turned out. Yesterday, a quick flip on the sewing machine produced some bunting made from a dress Ma had conjured up for the WW2 victory celebrations and some fabric produced for the 1951 Exhibition we had in our downstairs loo. Jimmy loves it and sits in the rocking chair given to us by Carole, looking on to the fields and beyond. It's comforting to see him relaxed and happy.

top: *Beef on the hoof and in need of a haircut*
bottom: *Carole's rocking chair in pride of place*

Trout with orange sauce

INGREDIENTS

1 rainbow trout fillet per person
1 heaped tbsp soft butter
grated zest of ½ orange
about 5 fresh thyme sprigs, leaves picked
salt and ground black pepper
a splash of white wine
1 scant tsp honey (I know this sounds odd with fish, but it works, trust me)

Preheat the oven to 200°C (180°C fan) mark 6. First of all, remove all the small bones left in the trout. I use a pair of tweezers but the tip of a pointed knife and your thumb work almost as well. |Lay the fish into a baking dish. Mix the butter with the orange zest, thyme leaves, salt and pepper and dot on top of the fish. Pour over the white wine and the honey and place in the oven for about 5 minutes, or until the fish is cooked. Serve with asparagus and buttered wholemeal bread.

right: *Trout and asparagus with orange sauce*

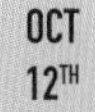

OCT 12TH

A really quick and nourishing soup – thick and creamy. It's a must on a frosty morning.

Golden soup

Heat a little oil or butter in a pan and add the onion, carrots and celery. Stir and sweat over a moderate heat for about 5 minutes. Add the stock and garlic, stir and bring to the boil. Reduce the heat and simmer until the vegetables are cooked, about 10 minutes.

Next, add the beans and bring back to the boil for about 2 minutes. Remove from the heat and blitz with a hand-held blender. Add the milk and season. Blitz again, check the seasoning and serve with a sprinkling of chopped parsley.

INGREDIENTS

about 1 tbsp oil or butter
1 large onion, finely chopped
2 large carrots, finely chopped
2 celery sticks, finely chopped
2½ cups chicken stock or stock made from a cube or concentrate
1–2 garlic cloves, crushed or chopped
400g (14oz) can cannellini beans, drained and rinsed
about 1½ cups milk
fresh parsley, chopped
salt and ground black pepper

left: *Golden evening sunshine on carrots and potatoes*

above: *My little 'flock'*

Hurry curry

INGREDIENTS

about 1 tbsp vegetable or sunflower oil
about 350–400g (10½–14oz) lamb neck fillet, cut into 1cm (½in) slices
1 large onion, finely sliced
½–¾ tsp ground cumin
½–¾ tsp ground turmeric
½–¾ tsp ground coriander
1 cinnamon stick, broken into pieces
½ tsp dried chilli flakes
2.5cm (1in) piece fresh root ginger, peeled and grated
1–2 garlic cloves, crushed or sliced
300–425ml (½–¾ pint) chicken stock (enough to just cover the meat and onions)
salt and ground black pepper

Heat the oil in a flameproof casserole over a high heat and brown the meat on both sides. If your casserole is small, do this in stages to avoid a soggy, grey mass. Lift the meat out and put in a bowl to one side.

Cook the onion for about 5 minutes in the same oil as the lamb until it begins to soften, but not take on colour. Add the spices, ginger and garlic, stir and cook for a further 2 minutes. Add the meat and any juices back to the pan, then add the stock. Bring to the boil, cover, reduce the heat and either simmer over a very low heat on top of the stove or cook in an oven preheated to 190°C (170°C fan) mark 5 for about 1½ hours, or until the meat is very tender.

Season to taste and serve with red lentil dhal (see opposite) and cucumber raita (see page 91).

Red lentil dhal

INGREDIENTS

1 cup red lentils, thoroughly washed

1 large garlic clove, crushed

salt

½ tsp cayenne pepper

1 tbsp vegetable or sunflower oil

1 large onion, very finely sliced

Bring the lentils to the boil in about 300–425ml (½–¾ pint) cold water, but do not add salt at this stage or the lentils will be tough. Reduce the heat and simmer until cooked, about 20 minutes. You need to stir them now and again, adding more water if necessary. When soft and beginning to turn mushy add the garlic, salt to taste and enough cayenne to give a little kick – the quantity is up to you.

Heat the oil in another pan, add the onion and fry until dark golden brown. Because this needs constant stirring I add a little water so that I can carry on doing other things: the onion will soften happily on its own and, once the water has evaporated you must return to the stove and stir until it is nicely browned. Put this on the lentils and serve either on its own with plain rice and/or with a curry.

OCT 15TH *When we were clearing the runner beans in the raised beds today we got the biggest surprise: a toad was preparing to hibernate underneath the oregano. He was a whopper!*

I have just made four pasties using some of the beef skirt I froze the other day. My mother never put anything other than chopped meat, potatoes and onion in pasties – definitely no turnip, swede or carrot – plus some salt and masses of pepper.

below: *Mr Toad*

OCT 16TH

Cornish pasties

INGREDIENTS

1 pack of read-rolled all butter puff or shortcrust pastry
225g (8oz) beef skirt, chopped by hand into tiny pieces
1 large onion, very finely chopped
1 large potato, peeled and very finely chopped
salt and lots of ground black pepper
1 egg, beaten

Preheat the oven to 200°C (180°C fan) mark 6. Cut the pastry into rounds using a saucer, then lay the meat and veg on one half of the round and season. Moisten the edges with beaten egg, fold in half and seal. Crimp the edges to make the classic pasty shape – if you can! I am all fingers and thumbs and don't manage a professional finish. Glaze the pasty with more of the egg wash and bake in the oven for about 25 minutes, or until the pastry is cooked and golden. One packet of pastry makes about 3 chunky pasties.

Secret supper

Foraged before nightfall.

INGREDIENTS

1 small potato
1 fat carrot
various salad leaves
radicchio
leftovers of a guinea fowl roasted yesterday (chicken would be ideal)

I ate the above with some runner bean chutney and mayo.

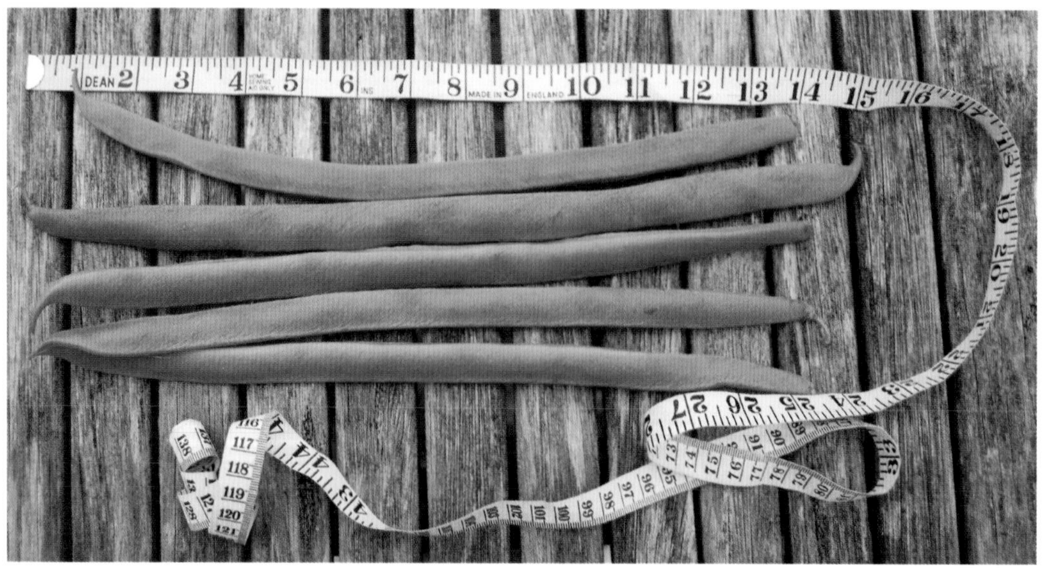

OCT 16TH

Oaty apple and raspberry crumble

INGREDIENTS

- 1 windfall Bramley apple, peeled and sliced
- a handful of raspberries, which have survived the frost

FOR THE CRUMBLE

- ¾ cup organic jumbo porridge oats
- ½ cup ground almonds
- a knob of butter
- 2 heaped tsp demerara sugar

Preheat the oven to 200°C (180°C fan) mark 6. Put the apple and raspberries into a small baking dish. Put the oats, almonds, butter and sugar into a mini-whizzer and quickly blitz – you don't want it to bind together but to remain crumbly. Put this on top of the fruit and bake in the oven for about 15 minutes. I dined like a prince... or a queen.

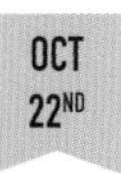
OCT 22ND

Pasta with olives and tomatoes

INGREDIENTS

- 1 red onion, finely chopped
- olive oil
- 1 small tub (from the deli section) of sundried and blush tomatoes and black olives
- 2 tomatoes, chopped
- 2 garlic cloves, crushed
- basil
- salt and ground black pepper
- red chilli, if you like
- freshly grated Parmesan cheese
- batch of cooked pasta of your choice, to serve

In a non-stick frying pan, sweat the onion in a good dash of olive oil for about 3 minutes over a moderate heat, then add the other ingredients, plus a little water. Simmer, stirring frequently, while the pasta is cooking. Serve with lots of freshly grated Parmesan.

above: *Apples ripening on the tree*

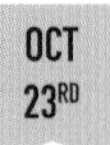

This is a nice soup for Bonfire Night for those who prefer to turn pumpkins into lanterns rather than eat them.

Watercress and butternut squash soup

INGREDIENTS

- olive oil
- 1 red onion, chopped
- 1 celery stick, finely sliced
- 2 cups chopped butternut squash
- 1 carrot, finely chopped
- 1 large potato, peeled and chopped
- 1 fat garlic clove, chopped
- 1 small red chilli, deseeded and chopped
- enough vegetable stock or water to cover the vegetables
- 1 standard bag of watercress
- 1½–2 cups milk
- salt and ground black pepper

Pour a small amount of oil into a pan and throw in the onion, celery, butternut squash, carrot and potato. Stir and sweat over a moderate heat for a few minutes, but don't allow to brown. Add the garlic and chilli, and enough stock or water to cover the vegetables. Bring to the boil, cover, then reduce the heat and simmer until the vegetables are soft, about 10 minutes. Add the watercress, stir and cook for a further 5 minutes.

Remove from the heat and blitz in the pan with a hand-held blender. Add some milk and blitz again. Taste and season.

TIP

You can use chicken stock instead of vegetable or water, and add a dash of cream at the end. This is a super soup, low calorie and packed with goodness – and above all, it tastes great.

right: *Watercress and butternut squash soup*

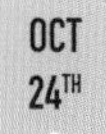

OCT 24TH

This makes a great side dish for bangers at Halloween.

Pumpkin and celeriac gratin

INGREDIENTS

1 small, firm pumpkin or wedge from a large one, peeled, deseeded and finely sliced
½ celeriac, peeled and finely sliced
1 garlic clove, finely chopped
150ml (¼ pint) single or double cream
a little milk
fresh nutmeg
salt and ground black pepper

Preheat the oven to 200°C (180°C fan) mark 6. Place the pumpkin and celeriac slices in layers in a shallow gratin dish, then sprinkle over the garlic. Mix the cream with a little milk and pour over the vegetables. Grate a small amount of fresh nutmeg (¼ tsp – no more or it will taste like rice pudding), season well and bake in the oven for about 30 minutes, or until bubbling and golden.

OCT 25TH

A day of contrasts which dawned freezing cold and frosty – the chickens' feathers were soaked having spent yet another night on the roof of the coop but still produced four eggs between them. By midday it was sunny and warm enough to have drinks in the garden with some friends who came for lunch.

right: *Red sky in the morning...*

above: *No sign yet of frosty nights*

Roast leg of lamb

INGREDIENTS

1 leg or shoulder of lamb
fresh rosemary sprigs, cut into little snips
2–3 garlic cloves, cut into slivers
salt and ground black pepper
1 onion, roughly chopped
2 celery sticks, sliced
juice of 1 lemon
olive oil

Normally I buy a shoulder joint but as we were going to be seven all with healthy appetites, the shoulders on offer were too small so I opted for a larger leg. Going up the simple route I used a sharp pointed knife and pierced the meat, then I inserted the rosemary and slivers of garlic into the slits, seasoning it well. I put the meat and vegetables into a large plastic bag with the lemon juice and a good slug of olive oil and sealed the bag. I massaged the meat pushing the marinade into all the nooks and crannies, then put the bag into the fridge for at least 1 hour.

I preheated the oven to 200°C (180°C fan) mark 6 and took the lamb out of the fridge 30 minutes before cooking to bring it to room temperature. I emptied everything into a roasting dish and cooked it in the oven for about 1½ hours depending on how you like your lamb.

The celery and onion caramelise during cooking and make a perfect gravy with the addition of a little vegetable stock or water.

Roasted vegetables

INGREDIENTS

Into a roasting dish went:
2 sweet potatoes, peeled and chopped
2 large carrots, cut into chunks
2–3 red onions, cut into quarters
1 each of red, orange and yellow peppers, deseeded and torn into large pieces
2 garlic cloves, skins on and squashed
a good splash of olive oil
salt and ground black pepper

Preheat the oven to 200°C (180°C fan) mark 6. Place everything in a roasting pan and roast in the oven for about 45 minutes.

Gratin dauphinois

INGREDIENTS

450–675g (1–1½lb) potatoes, peeled and finely sliced
2 garlic cloves, sliced
1 large tub crème fraîche or 1¼ cups double cream
½ pint (300ml) milk
fresh nutmeg
salt and ground black pepper
butter

Preheat the oven to 200°C (180°C fan) mark 6. Put the potatoes into a shallow baking dish with the garlic. Mix the crème fraîche or double cream with enough milk to make it like single cream, then pour over the potatoes, grating a little nutmeg over the top. Season, dot with butter and bake in the oven for about 45 minutes–1 hour until bubbling and golden.

Apple crumble

INGREDIENTS

450g (1lb) apples peeled and sliced
1 heaped tbsp demerara sugar (to be used with the raw apples; if using cookers, add a little more sugar)
½ lemon

FOR THE TOPPING

85g (3oz) slightly salted butter
1 cup porridge oats
½ cup ground almonds
½ cup plain flour
1 heaped tbsp demerara sugar

Preheat the oven to 200°C (180°C fan) mark 6. Lay the apples in a medium shallow baking dish and sprinkle with 1 heaped tsp of the demerara sugar, then grate over the lemon zest.

Whizz the butter, oats, ground almonds and flour in bursts in a food processor – you don't want it to bind together but to remain crumbly, then add the remaining sugar and blitz quickly once more. Bake in the oven for about 25–30 minutes until the top is golden brown and the fruit cooked. Serve with custard, vanilla ice cream… or clotted cream… or all three.

below: *The year is not yet over*

above: *You know where to find me*

Hot topped chicken breast

INGREDIENTS

1 chicken breast per person
For each chicken breast you will need:
1 cup fresh brown breadcrumbs
either ½ fresh red chilli, deseeded and chopped small or a pinch dried chilli flakes
finely grated zest of ½ large or 1 small lemon
2 tbsp olive oil
salt and ground black pepper

Preheat the oven to 200°C (180°C fan) mark 6. Skin your chicken breast(s) and place in a shallow baking dish. Mix all the other ingredients together in a bowl and spread on top of the chicken. Bake in the oven until the juices run clear. You can moisten the dish with a little water, stock or white wine to make a gravy.

Serve with mashed potato or plain basmati rice and vegetables.

TIP

Double the quantities and use it to cover a spatchcocked whole chicken. To spatchcock a bird, place it on a board and thump down on the breastbone with your flat hand. Turn the chicken over and cut all the way along the spine using special chicken shears or strong kitchen scissors. Cut away the backbone and discard. Open up the bird, turn it over, skin-side up, and flatten again. Place in a baking dish and spoon or smear the mixture on top. Drizzle with a little more olive oil and bake in a hot oven for about 1¼ hours depending on the weight, or until the juices run clear. Serve with a green salad made with a butterhead lettuce and a light dressing.

Sometimes chicken breasts can be a touch dry. This simple curry comes straight from the hills in Shimla or the Muthaiga Club in Nairobi.

Raj style chicken curry with fruit

INGREDIENTS

- Leftover cold chicken picked from the carcass
- 1 onion, cut into quarters
- 1 carrot, sliced
- 1 celery stick
- 1 crispy apple
- juice of ½ lemon
- 30g (1oz) ghee (clarified butter) or 1–2 tbsp sunflower oil
- 1 onion, sliced
- 1 tbsp mild curry powder
- ½ green pepper, deseeded and cut into small chunks
- ½ cup sultanas
- 1 garlic clove, chopped
- 1¼ cups chicken stock
- salt and ground black pepper

Put the carcass and chicken bones, plus the quartered onion, the sliced carrot and stick of celery into a saucepan, barely cover with water and bring to the boil. Reduce the heat and simmer for 15 minutes. Strain and keep to one side.

Remove the core and pips from the apple but not the skin and chop into small pieces, and place the apple pieces in a bowl of water with lemon juice added to stop the apple going brown. Heat the ghee or oil in a pan over a moderate–high heat – I find a wok with a lid works really well – and add the sliced onion. Cook, stirring frequently, until soft and beginning to take on some colour. Add the curry powder and fry quickly for a minute. Add the green pepper, leftover chicken, sultanas, garlic and apple to the onion. Pour in the chicken stock, season with salt and pepper and bring to the boil. Cover the pan or wok and reduce the heat to a gentle bubble while you cook some plain basmati rice. Serve with cucumber raita (see page 91) and some mango chutney.

TIP

If there was no mango chutney in the house, my great-great grandmother used to mix apricot jam with a good dash of Worcestershire sauce – it became a family standby

NOV 1ST

One-pan chicken with potatoes

INGREDIENTS

a little sunflower oil
1 whole chicken leg per person
1 potato per person, peeled and chopped into smallish pieces
1 garlic clove, chopped or grated
juice of ½ lemon or a whole one if cooking for more than 2
glass or two of white wine
salt and ground black pepper
½ tub crème fraîche

Heat the oil in a pan and brown the chicken pieces on both sides – don't rush this. Add the chopped potato, garlic, lemon juice, wine and season with salt and pepper. Bring to the boil, cover, reduce the heat and simmer for about 15–20 minutes. You may have to add a little more liquid during cooking, either more white wine or water. When the chicken is thoroughly cooked, add a good half of a tub of crème fraîche, stir well and bring back to the boil. Reduce the heat and simmer a further 5 minutes and serve.

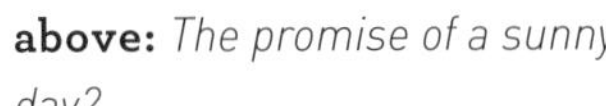

above: *The promise of a sunny day?*

TIP

If you are concerned that it all looks rather pale and uninteresting, sprinkle over some freshly chopped parsley before serving.

NOV 2ND

Now that the cold weather is finally beginning to show its teeth I made this light, delicate apple pudding.

Apple pudding

Preheat the oven to 200°C (180°C fan) mark 6. Gently stew the apples with the soft brown sugar and 1 tbsp water in a saucepan until mushy, then tip into medium baking dish to cool. Cream the butter and caster sugar in a bowl with a wooden spoon or use hand-held electric beaters until light and fluffy, then gradually beat in the eggs. Fold in the almonds and pour on to the cooked apple. Cook in the oven for 30 minutes, or until the sponge is golden brown.

TIP

To vary flavours, sometimes I slice a few strawberries on top of the cooked apple or stir in a little grated zest of lemon/orange before adding the sponge batter.

INGREDIENTS

2 large cooking apples (675g/1½lb), peeled and sliced
55g (2oz) soft brown sugar or 50/50 demerara sugar
115g (4oz) soft butter
115g (4oz) caster sugar
2 large eggs, beaten
115g (4oz) ground almonds

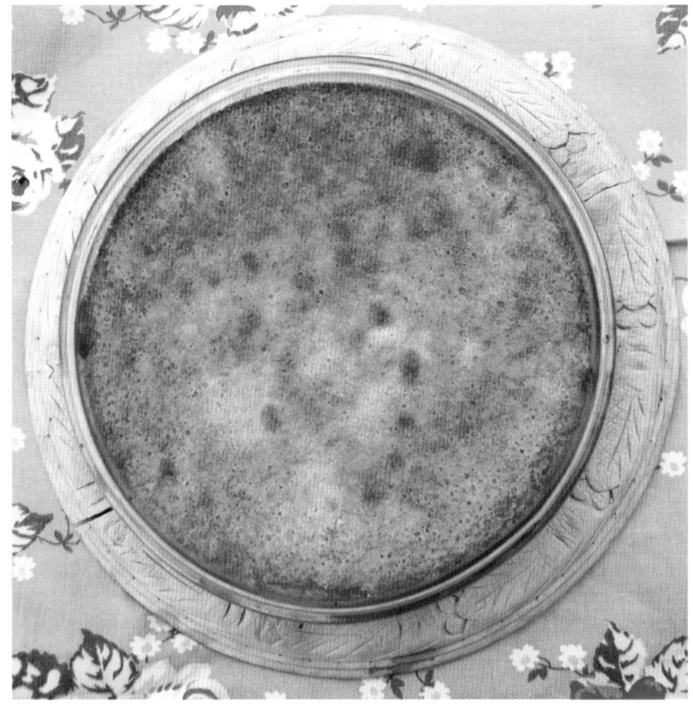

left: *Apple pudding*

This is a very nice and unusual accompaniment to a roast.

Braised leeks and fennel

INGREDIENTS
1 large fennel bulb, finely sliced
2 leeks, finely sliced
olive oil
salt and ground black pepper
1 cup chicken stock, if you like

Preheat the oven to 200°C (180°C fan) mark 6. Place the fennel and leeks in a baking dish. Stir in a drizzle of olive oil and season well. Sometimes I moisten it with a little chicken stock. Cook in the oven for about 20 minutes.

right: *Ready for the pot*

above: *Trouble in store*

NOV 11TH *Today's weather has been like the end of the world. The only antidote was to go into the kitchen and bake my heart out. I wanted a major sugar rush but with no fuss and no bother, and this is what I came up with.*

Fairy cakes surprise

INGREDIENTS

- 1 large egg
- caster sugar (same weight as egg)
- butter (same weight as egg)
- self-raising flour (same weight as egg)
- ¼ tsp baking powder
- little milk if needed
- raspberry jam

I preheated the oven to 200°C (180°C fan) mark 6. I took one lovely brown egg and weighed it (in its shell) – it was just over 55g (2oz). I then weighed the same amount of caster sugar, some very soft, slightly salted butter and self-raising flour. I put them into a bowl, cracked in the egg and added a good pinch (¼ tsp) baking powder. It all came together in seconds. You want the mix to drop off a spoon, not stay put, so you may need to add a little milk.

I spooned a small amount (about a third of the way up) into 4–5 muffin cases and then added a good tsp of homemade raspberry jam. I then topped with more cake mix and put them in the oven for about 10 minutes, or until they were golden brown and the point of a knife came out clean. I left them to cool and then dusted them with a little more caster sugar. The jam had mixed in with some of the cake and it was like biting into a light, fluffy doughnut.

TIP

It doesn't matter what filling you use; lemon curd would be nice and, if so, add a little lemon zest to the raw cake mix.

My one egg made five little cakes.

I did my usual by buying a free-range organic whole chicken (reduced), cutting it up into pieces and freezing what I didn't need for another day.

Chicken breasts with cream cheese and Parma ham

INGREDIENTS
cream cheese
1 garlic clove, chopped
basil leaves, torn
1 chicken breast per person
1–2 slices Parma ham per chicken breast
salt and ground black pepper
olive oil
1 small glass of white wine

Preheat the oven to 200°C (180°C fan) mark 6. Depending on how many chicken breasts you are preparing, mix the cream cheese (about 1 tbsp per breast) with the garlic and torn basil leaves and put into the cavity of the chicken breasts (skins removed first). Wrap them in the Parma ham and put them into a shallow baking dish, then season with salt and lots of pepper, a dash of olive oil and the white wine. Bake in the oven until the juices run clear.

Serve with something green and mashed sweet potato to which is added a large knob of butter, salt and ground black pepper and some freshly grated nutmeg.

right: *A night on the tiles*

NOV 15TH

Having eaten the chicken breasts I was left with the frozen legs and thighs.

Easy risotto

INGREDIENTS

2½–5 cups hot stock (preferably chicken but vegetable is fine)
sunflower oil
1 small onion, finely chopped
6 nice fat spears asparagus, cut into 2.5cm (1in) long pieces
1 red pepper, deseeded and chopped into small chunks
1 cup frozen petits pois
4 small spring onions, sliced
2 garlic cloves, crushed
arborio rice (special rice for risotto), about 75g (2¾oz) raw rice per serving
30g (1oz) butter
1 glass of white wine
a few fresh thyme sprigs, leaves picked (about ½ tsp)
Parmesan cheese

Keep the stock on a gentle heat. Start by putting a little oil in a large, flat pan – I use one which is about 25cm (10in) across and 7.5cm (3in) deep. Add the onion and cook for about 5 minutes, stirring every now and again. Add the vegetables, including the garlic and thyme, and stir. Cook a further 2 minutes. Add the rice and butter, a cupful of stock and the wine, and stir. Cook for 5 minutes, stirring every now and again so that the bottom doesn't stick. Now comes the 'work' bit: keep stirring, keeping the pan on a gentle bubble. The rice will absorb the hot stock as it cooks, so add more gradually, stirring as you go. You will be surprised just how much stock is needed. If you run out continue with hot water from the kettle. When most of the liquid has been absorbed, the rice is cooked how you like it and the feel of the risotto is creamy and rich (I suppose this took about 30–40 minutes), grate some fresh Parmesan on top, then check the seasoning and adjust accordingly.

Serve in hot bowls. Some people like a little 'bite' to their rice but as with pasta, I don't like to feel that the centre is raw and possibly cook mine longer than the norm.

above: *Scotch eggs*

Scotch eggs

INGREDIENTS

- 4 hard-boiled eggs
- 1 pack of high quantity meat/ best quality pork sausages
- 1 tsp dried mixed herbs
- flour
- fresh breadcrumbs or Panko crumbs
- 1 extra egg
- low-calorie oil spray for baking

Preheat the oven to 200°C (180°C fan) mark 6. I put the eggs on to boil and after about 8 minutes, ran them under the cold tap and removed the shells. I squeezed the sausage meat from the casings into a bowl adding the dried mixed herbs and mixing it with my bare hands.

Wrapping the eggs with the sausage meat can be a messy business but, if you follow this tip, it is so much easier: divide the sausage meat into four equal portions. Tear off a piece of clingfilm and put a lump of meat on to one-half of the clingfilm, then fold over and smooth out with a rolling pin until it is large enough to wrap around each egg. Put a spoonful of flour into a dish and roll each egg in it. Then, peel back the clingfilm and place the egg on top of the flattened sausage meat. Close the clingfilm/sausage meat around the egg and gently ease it so that the egg is sealed inside. Remove the clingfilm and repeat the process until all four eggs are covered.

Next, add more flour to the bowl if needed, put the fresh breadcrumbs or Panko crumbs into another bowl and crack the remaining egg into a third bowl beating it lightly. Dip each Scotch egg first into the flour, then in the egg and then into the breadcrumbs. You can, of course, shallow-fry these, but I prefer to spray them with a low-calorie oil and cook them in the oven on a baking tray for about 20 minutes, or until the sausage meat is cooked through and golden brown.

Serve cold with freshly made English mustard, your own chutney, spring onions and salad.

TIP

Don't forget: left hand 'dry', right hand 'wet' when coating with egg and breadcrumbs

NOV 18TH *Why not use a bag of frozen berries to make some jam for a treat on a cold afternoon? You will be able to enjoy a pot of fresh-tasting preserve in time for the weekend to sandwich between the layers of a Victoria sponge cake or with warm scones and clotted cream. I am a cream-first, jam-second girl when it comes to scones – the cream in the place of butter.*

Out of season berry jam

INGREDIENTS
frozen mixed fruit
equal quantity of jam sugar with pectin

Put a small metal dish or saucer in the icebox or freezer and sterilise your jars in a warm oven for 15 minutes (see page 5). There's no need to thaw the fruit first; pour it into a pan with the same weight of sugar. There should be no need to add any extra water as the ice around the fruit should suffice. Gently bring to the boil, stirring as you go to dissolve the sugar, and allow it to bubble away until it reaches setting point: test a small amount on the chilled dish. When the jam is ready, pour into the hot jars, seal and label.

NOV 22ND *Christmas will be upon us in a month and I am fat. There is more of me out of the bath water than in it. I am definitely not a rock chick, rocky rocky, rock chick – more of a rock cake, rocky rocky, rock cake and would probably fetch three camels, a goat and a sheep in the souk. Make that four camels.*

above: *Little beauties*
below: *Nymph on a plinth*

top: *Ready to attack the mites in the chicken coop – a wake-up call*
bottom: My watercolour of Barcaldine Castle, Argyll and Bute

Never trust a skinny cook. It's diet time. NOTE TO SELF:

- *Don't put anything into the trolley that is going to make me fatter.*
- *Don't shop for food when I am hungry.*
- *Breakfast: porridge made with water, a little semi-skimmed milk and our honey or blueberries.*
- *Lunch: homemade soup and/or salad.*
- *If peckish drink a glass of water, have a piece of fruit or eat a dab of toothpaste.*
- *Supper: lots and lots of veg, either in stir-fry (using low calorie spray) or grilled fish or meat – eat one chop rather than two and NEVER crispy chicken skin.*
- *No bread, no butter, no cheese, no custard, no cream, no fun.*

Great uncle Alec's* kitcheree

INGREDIENTS

1 smoked, undyed haddock fillet
enough milk to poach the fish
2 bay leaves
1 cup cooked basmati rice
3 large potatoes, cooked and sliced when cold
lots of butter
salt and ground black pepper
lots of cayenne pepper
fresh parsley, chopped

Preheat the oven to 200°C (180°C fan) mark 6. Gently poach the haddock (adjust the quantity to the number of mouths to feed) in milk with the bay leaves for 10 minutes, or until cooked. Remove the skin and bones from the fish and flake the flesh, keep some of the milk to one side. Place the fish, rice and potatoes in layers in a shallow baking dish and dot liberally with butter, adding some of the reserved cooking liquor. Season with salt, pepper and quite a lot of cayenne, then cover with foil and heat through in the oven for 15 to 20 minutes or until piping hot.

Serve with more butter and lots and lots of chopped parsley.

* Sir Alexander Campbell, 4th Baronet of Barcaldine and Glenure

Mixed vegetables and sweet potato soup

Add 1 pint of boiling water to the concentrated chicken stock cube or jelly pot and put everything into a large saucepan, with enough water to cover, and simmer for 10–15 minutes until soft. Blitz in a blender or using a hand-held blender.

This is perfect for a chilly day. I completed the picture with croutons made from two slices of Vogel's bread and olive oil.

INGREDIENTS

- 1 sweet potato, peeled and cut into chunks
- 1 large red onion, peeled and sliced
- 1 red, orange or yellow pepper, de-seeded and cut into small chunks
- 2 celery sticks, sliced
- 2 large garlic cloves, peeled and chopped
- 1 red chilli, de-seeded and finely sliced with seeds, or if more heat required, include the seeds
- 3 large tomatoes skins and all
- a few fresh thyme sprigs
- drizzle of olive oil
- salt and ground black pepper
- 1 chicken stock cube or jelly pot

left: *Mixed roasted vegetables and sweet potato soup*

NOV 30TH

Crunchy red slaw

INGREDIENTS

1 tbsp flaked almonds
¼ red cabbage, finely shredded or sliced
1 large carrot, grated
1 red onion, sliced
1 fennel bulb, finely sliced
1 tbsp pumpkin seeds
1 tbsp sunflower seeds
1 crunchy apple, skin on and cut into chunks
1 garlic clove, crushed

FOR THE DRESSING

1 tbsp natural yogurt
1 tsp French mustard
juice of ½ lemon
1 tbsp cider vinegar
1 tbsp olive oil
salt and ground black pepper

This will keep a couple of days in the fridge – great with cold meat and poultry over Christmas.

Heat a small frying pan over a moderate heat and lightly toast the flaked almonds. Watch these like a hawk or they will burn. Add to the other salad ingredients. Whisk together the ingredients for the dressing and pour on to the salad, mixing well. It doesn't matter a bit as to quantities and you can always add some fresh herbs if you wish. To make a light lunch with added protein I topped it with one of the girls' eggs, hard-boiled and sliced.

right: *Crunchy red slaw*

Pork casserole with cannellini beans

INGREDIENTS

225g (8oz) shoulder of pork, cut into small cubes
olive oil
1–2 carrots, sliced
1 leek, sliced
1 onion, sliced
400g (14oz) cannellini beans or any other beans you fancy, canned, drained and rinsed
grated zest and juice of ½ lemon
1 bay leaf
a few fresh thyme sprigs
1 tbsp concentrated tomato purée
425ml (¾ pint) chicken stock
1 garlic clove, crushed

Preheat the oven to 200°C (180°C fan) mark 6. In a flameproof casserole, brown the pork in a little oil over a high heat. Add all the other ingredients, stir and bring to the boil. Simmer in the oven for about 1–1½ hours until the meat is very tender. You may need to top up with more stock or a little water during cooking. Serve with a sprinkling of chopped parsley and a bowl of good old mashed buttery spuds.

left: *Fresh borlotti beans*

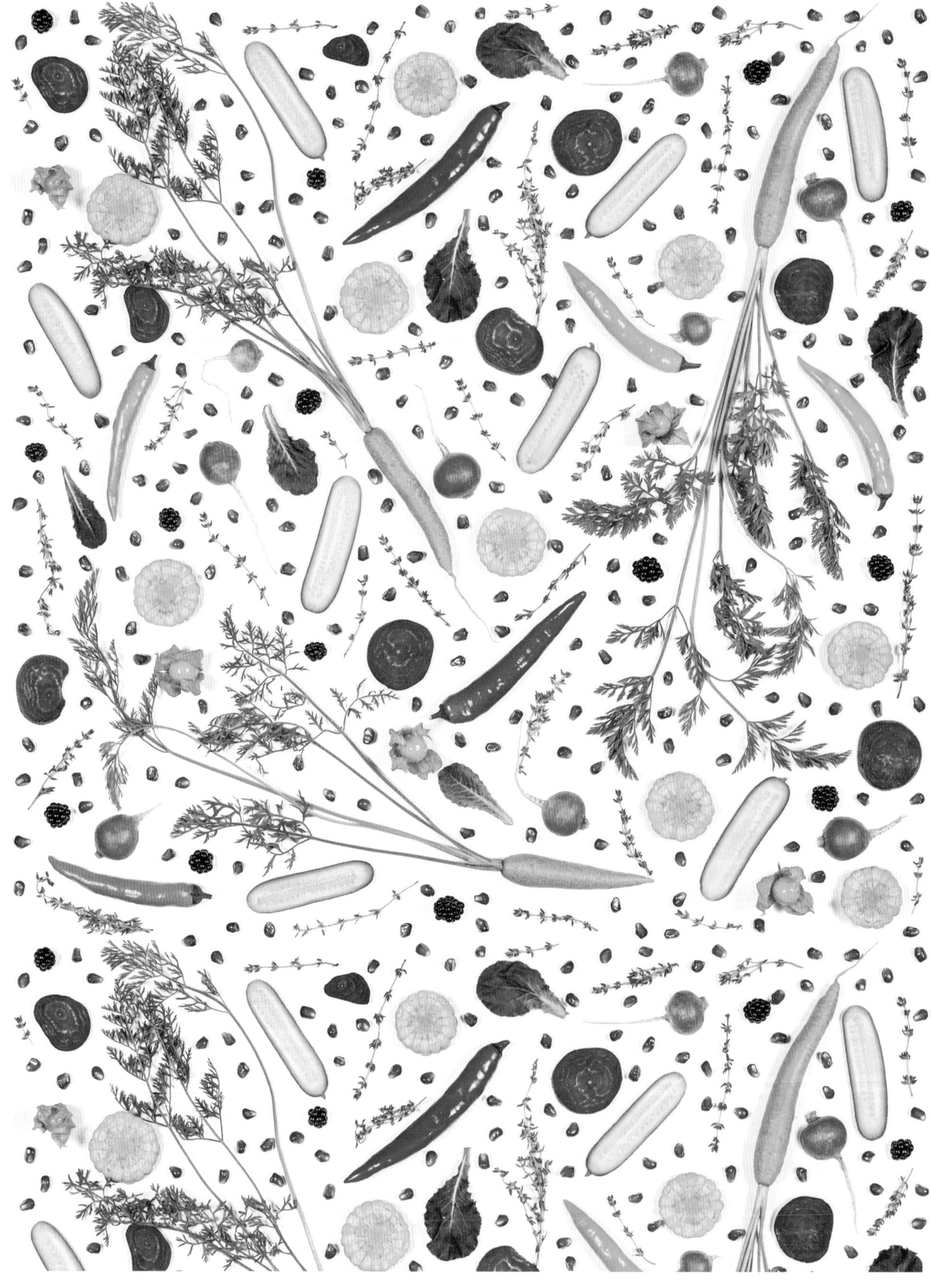

WINTER

DEC 2ND

I love these Mexican style eggs; they kick start a 'chilli' day perfectly.

Mexican eggs

Heat a non-stick frying pan over a moderate-high heat and fry the onion in the oil for about 5 minutes, stirring to prevent burning. Add the tomatoes and chilli and cook for a further 2 minutes or so before adding the beans. Mix and cook over a low-moderate heat until the onions and tomatoes are soft. Part the vegetables in the centre of the pan and crack in the egg. Place a lid on the pan and cook gently until the white is set, and the yolk runny. Season with salt and pepper and serve immediately sprinkled with fresh coriander.

INGREDIENTS

1 red onion, chopped very small
2 tsp vegetable or sunflower oil
1–2 tomatoes, finely chopped
1 fresh green or red chilli (with seeds if you want extra heat), or a pinch of dried chilli flakes
400g (14oz) can black beans, drained and rinsed
1 egg
salt and ground black pepper
fresh coriander leaves

above: *Mexican eggs – not the prettiest but a great start to the day*
right: *Chilli fest*

DEC 7TH

At last I have ticked one wish off my bucket list and have been to Dungeness to see the late Derek Jarman's cottage and his iconic garden. I loved the isolation of the area, the sense of out-of-this-worldliness and the skyline, the trip culminating in fish and chips at the Pilot Inn. I took the pretty road back home, travelling through woodland and forests down country lanes resplendent in a metallic kaleidoscope of bronze, copper and gold. An added bonus in travelling west was the magnificent sunset, the crowning glory of a wonderful day.

Rustled up this quick soup for a friend who has been poorly but fit enough to join me for lunch today.

Butternut squash soup

INGREDIENTS

3 slices butternut squash, peeled and cut into chunks
1 sweet potato, peeled and cut into chunks
1 carrot, sliced
1 onion, sliced
1 celery stick, sliced
2½ cups chicken or vegetable stock
olive oil
salt and ground black pepper
sprinkle of dried chilli flakes
1 cup milk
1 tbsp fresh coriander, chopped

Put everything, except the milk and coriander, into a saucepan, bring to the boil and stir. Reduce the heat and simmer for about 15 minutes, or until the vegetables are soft. Blitz with a hand-held blender, then adjust the seasoning, add the milk and coriander leaves and quickly whizz again before serving.

top: *Derek Jarman's cottage*
bottom: *On guard duty*

above: *Pretty green plate, pretty as a picture*

Leftover chicken and green peppers

INGREDIENTS

1 leek, roughly chopped
1 green pepper, deseeded and finely sliced
olive oil
Leftover cold chicken cut into small pieces (skin and bones removed)
finely grated zest and juice of ½ lemon
1 garlic clove, crushed
400g (14oz) can butter beans, drained and rinsed
a pinch of dried chilli flakes
soy sauce
300 ml (½ pt) chicken stock

Sweat the leek and pepper in a dash of oil in a wok over a moderate heat for 3 minutes, stirring all the while. Add the chicken, lemon zest and juice, garlic, butter beans, chilli flakes and a good splash of soy. Moisten with the chicken stock and serve piping hot in a bowl with a chunk of crunchy sourdough bread. Wholesome, hearty and delicious.

Steamed fillets of sea bream

INGREDIENTS

1 sea bream fillet per person

For each fillet you will need:
1 or 2 spring onions, sliced
piece fresh root ginger, sliced (about the thickness of a pound coin)
1 garlic clove, sliced
3 tbsp soy sauce

Place the fillet(s) on a plate along with the spring onions, ginger, garlic and soy, then place in a steamer and steam for about 5–7 minutes. Serve with steamed spinach, potatoes and courgettes. Cooked this way you can really appreciate the delicate freshness of the fish.

DEC 18TH

In the past, I have cooked several different Christmas cake recipes but I felt like a complete change. The hens laid three eggs this week – a miracle, bearing in mind the terrible weather, which has not been conducive to sitting in the coop.

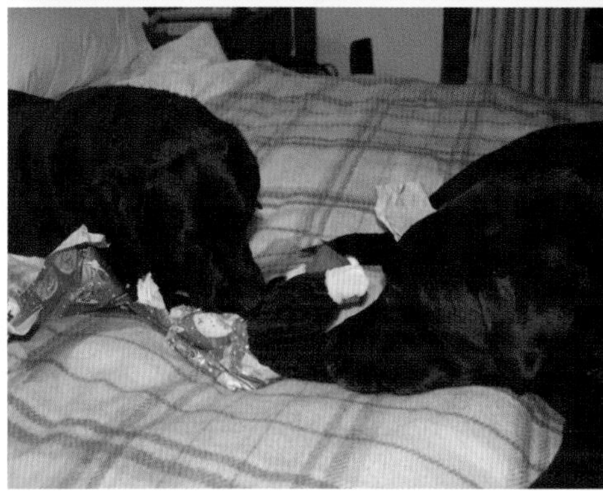

above: *How quickly the year has gone...*
below: *Suzie and best friend Toby opening their presents*

An alternative Christmas cake

INGREDIENTS
175g (6oz) salted butter plus extra for greasing
175g (6oz) caster sugar
3 eggs
175g (6oz) self-raising flour (sifted)
1 tsp baking powder (sifted)
10 natural glacé cherries, cut into quarters
grated zest and juice of 1 orange
1 tsp mixed spice
3oz (85g) sultanas

FOR THE ICING
4oz (500g) icing sugar
juice of 1 lemon

Preheat the oven to 200°C (180°C fan) mark 6. Butter a kugelhopf cake tin and put to one side. Bring the butter to room temperature and cream with the sugar until light and fluffy. Crack the eggs into a bowl and lightly beat. Add half the eggs plus 1 tbsp flour into the creamed butter and sugar. Beat well. Add the remaining egg mixture and mix well. Sieve the remaining flour and baking powder together. Fold in the sieved flour, the cherries, orange zest and juice, mixed spice and sultanas. Pour the batter into the prepared cake tin and bake in the middle of the oven for about 30 minutes, or until risen, golden brown and the skewer comes out clean.

Remove the cake from the oven, cover with a clean cloth and allow to cool for 10 minutes. Run a knife around the edge, tap firmly on a work surface and up-end on to a plate. Cover again with the cloth and allow to cool before icing.

Sift the icing sugar into a bowl and add the lemon juice. Beat to remove any lumps until creamy, then drizzle over the cake. The end result was crumbly, salty, buttery, fruity and spicy; exactly what you want at this time of the year and Jimmy, Neil and I almost finished it off in one go.

above: *Some like it hot*

DEC 15TH

This hot pepper jelly is a must, not only for Christmas but at any time of the year. It can be used to glaze roast duckling or grilled duck breasts, mixed with pork spare ribs or on top of cheese on toast - my particular favourite.

Hot pepper jelly

INGREDIENTS

4 large peppers (green, red, orange or yellow), deseeded
8 or more chillies (depending on how hot you want the jelly to be)
1½ cups cider vinegar
1kg (2¼lb) jam sugar with added pectin

First, having removed the seeds from the peppers, break them into chunks and blitz in a food processor taking care you don't totally pulverise them, then put them into a large pan. Place a few jars into a warm oven to sterilise (see page 5).

Pulse the chillies (seeds removed first if you don't want too much heat) and add to the peppers along with the vinegar. Stir and bring to the boil over a high heat – the fumes will be strong and will probably make you cough. Reduce the heat slightly and cook for 5 minutes. Put a small metal dish or saucer into the freezer.

Add the sugar to the pan and stir, making sure it is all dissolved. Cook for about 5–8 minutes until it reaches setting point, but check the instructions on the sugar pack first. Test a little on the chilled metal dish or saucer and if, when cold, it wrinkles when you run your finger through it, pour into the hot jars, seal and label. This is such a pretty jelly and the coloured pepper pieces sparkle like rubies and emeralds.

DEC 18TH

As a child I always knew that Christmas was around the corner when Ma brought out her large glass sweetie jar from the back of the cupboard and gave it a good wash. She used it to store a family favourite, Swedish pickle. This is so easy to prepare and can last several weeks in a cool, dark place or (in smaller jars) in the fridge. It is a perfect accompaniment to cold meats or in a cheese sandwich.

top: *The season to be merry*
bottom: *Swedish Christmas card (1950)*

Swedish pickle

INGREDIENTS

1 white cabbage, finely shredded
3 large carrots, finely grated
4 green peppers, deseeded and thinly sliced
450g (1lb) white onions, finely sliced
¼ cup salt
4 cups white wine or cider vinegar
2¼ cups granulated sugar

Mix all the vegetables together in a large bowl with the salt. Cover and leave overnight.

Next day, wash thoroughly under a cold running tap, drain and squeeze out as much of the water as you can. Heat 4 cups water, the vinegar and sugar in a large saucepan until the latter is fully dissolved. Set aside to cool. When it is cold pour over the vegetables, mix well and place in a large clean glass jar or plastic container with a lid. It's ready to eat straightaway.

HOME-MADE SNOW

It sparkles and shines in the warmest room as long as you want it

A glittering fir tree, crusted with snow, a crib, its roof weighed down by a white blanket —it's all done with soapflakes, or detergent would do as well. Soapflake snow looks exactly like the real thing, is quick to make and apply, lasts for months.

Empty half a packet of soapflakes into a bowl and add a little hot water. Whisk well for two minutes (an ordinary egg whisk or electric whisker is quickest), adding more soapflakes and hot water as needed to get an almost solid lather, with the consistency of really thick whipped cream.

Make sure the branches of your tree are completely dry. Using a teaspoon for a tiny tree, a tablespoon, or even hands, for a bigger one, apply the 'snow' along the branches, keeping in mind for a really natural effect that snow would not settle on hidden branches. If necessary, make more 'snow' in the same way. Scatter *dry* soapflakes lightly over the whole tree for extra sparkle. Leave for a day or two.

When thoroughly dry, your Christmas tree will glitter with crisp snowy spangles. Used on and around a crib, soapflake snow makes a firm foundation from which tiny holly 'bushes' and ivy sprays can grow.

Whisk well for the softest 'snow'

Apply along the tops of branches

top: *Ma's recipe for artificial snow*
bottom: *The stuffing in the making*

DEC 24TH

I found this card which I made last year and forgot to send. The recipe for 'snow' came from one of my mother's collection of Good Housekeeping *magazines dating from 1949, and she made it every year at Christmas to decorate our tree, adding a tiny drop or two of blue food colouring, which made it whiter. She used a whisk with a handle, which turned the blades and I can still smell the intoxicating mixture of lux flakes and pine needles. If we had any, she would dust the 'snow' while wet with silver glitter which sparkled when the fairy lights were lit. On Twelfth Night after taking down the decorations we put the tree outside and hosed away the soapy snow before planting it in the garden.*

Abandoning turkey this year we decided on roast duck. I raided the fridge to see what I could turn into a stuffing:

Roast duck with brown bread stuffing

INGREDIENTS
1 oven-ready duck

FOR THE STUFFING
2 shallots, finely sliced
1 celery stick, finely sliced
55g (2oz) butter
1 large Bramley apple, peeled, cored and chopped
1 nectarine, skin on, cut into small chunks
1 thick slice wholemeal bread, whizzed into crumbs
finely grated zest of 1 orange
a handful of fresh parsley, roughly chopped
salt and ground black pepper

Preheat the oven to 220°C (200°C fan) mark 7.

To make the stuffing, sweat the shallots and celery in the butter in a pan over a moderate heat for 5–6 minutes until soft. Once cool, mix with the apple, nectarine, breadcrumbs, orange zest and parsley. Season well, then pack it into the cavity of the bird. Roast in the oven for at least 1¼–1½ hours allowing some extra cooking time because of the stuffing. It was one of the nicest accompaniments I have tasted – and so easy to put together.

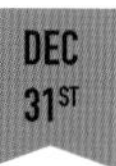

DEC 31ST

Beetroot and celeriac gratin

INGREDIENTS

2–3 small raw beetroot, peeled and finely sliced
same amount of celeriac, peeled and finely sliced
1 garlic clove, crushed
butter
salt and ground black pepper
150ml (¼ pint) double cream
1 cup milk
fresh chives, chopped

Preheat the oven to 200°C (180°C fan) mark 6. Lay the beetroot and celeriac in layers in a buttered shallow baking dish. Sprinkle with the garlic, season with salt and pepper and pour over enough double cream mixed with the milk to cover. Bake in the oven until bubbling and cooked through. Scatter with chopped chives. This would make a great side dish to a roast or as a light lunch with a bowl of green salad.

The house smells of freshly baked bread. Is it too early for tea?

above: *Perfectly formed globes of goodness*
left: *Hot off the press*

King prawn noodles Singapore-style

INGREDIENTS

1 pack of fresh raw King prawns
1 fresh red chilli, chopped (with or without the seeds depending on how hot you want it to be)
1 garlic clove, grated
about 2.5cm (1in) piece fresh root ginger, peeled and grated
juice of 1 lemon
1 tbsp soy sauce
2 nests of fine dried egg noodles
½ pepper (green, red, orange or yellow), deseeded and sliced
1 fennel bulb, finely sliced
vegetable oil
1 level tsp mild curry powder
4–6 spring onions, chopped
fresh coriander leaves, chopped

Carefully remove any remaining black intestinal veins running along the backs of the prawns, then put them in a bowl with a marinade made from the chilli, garlic, ginger, lemon juice and soy. Marinate for half an hour.

Cook a couple of nests of egg noodles according to the pack instructions, then rinse under cold water and set aside.

When ready to eat, heat a wok over a high heat and stir-fry the peppers and fennel in a little oil for 5 minutes. Add the prawns and marinade and stir-fry for 3 minutes, or until they turn pink. Add a splash of water, cover with a lid and cook in the steam for 2 minutes. Tip into a bowl. Add a little more oil to the wok, then add the curry powder and stir. Cook for a minute, then add the noodles and vegetables and another good splash of soy. Stir until thoroughly hot, sprinkle with chopped spring onions and fresh coriander leaves and serve.

right: *The raw prawns marinating*

JAN 9TH

Our wedding anniversary. Happy day.

Crispy stir-fried belly of pork

above: *Our wedding day, 9th January, 1991*

INGREDIENTS

2–3 lean slices belly of pork
cider vinegar
salt
4–6 spring onions
1 nest of rice noodles per person
vegetable or sunflower oil
4–6 spring greens, sliced
½ yellow pepper, de-seeded and sliced
1 large leek, sliced
1 celery stick, chopped
small head broccoli, sliced
1 courgette, cut into matchsticks
1 small fennel bulb, finely sliced
garlic clove, chopped or grated
2.5cm (1in) piece fresh root ginger, peeled and grated

Preheat the oven to 200°C (180°C fan) mark 6. Brush the pork skin with the cider vinegar – this will make the crackling 'crackle'. Sprinkle with salt and roast in the oven for about 40 minutes, or until the juices run clear. Rest the meat before slicing into small chunks. I found it easier to remove the crackling first and cut this up with scissors.

To turn the spring onions into Chinese-style decorations, use a pointed knife to carefully slice through the white part lengthways twice, then put into a glass of very cold water. This will make the onions fan out like an old-fashioned swizzle stick.

Cook the rice noodles according to the pack instructions, then rinse under the cold tap and put to one side. Heat the wok over a high heat, add 1 tsp oil and add the vegetables, garlic and ginger. Stir-fry, then cover with a lid for a further 3 minutes before adding the rice noodles. When the noodles have heated through (about 1 minute) serve in pretty soup bowls with some of the cooking juices. Lay the crispy pork on top and decorate with the spring onions.

JAN 10TH

Easy spinach roulade

INGREDIENTS

1 large pack of spinach
2 medium-large eggs
salt and ground black pepper
fresh nutmeg
2 tsp plain flour
15g (½oz) butter
150ml (¼ pint) milk
1 cup grated Gruyère cheese
1 tbsp crème fraîche
1 heaped tsp Dijon mustard
1 tbsp grated Parmesan cheese

Preheat the oven to 200°C (180°C fan) mark 6. Thoroughly wash the spinach, shake off excess water and place in a pan to cook quickly, stirring until it is wilted. Remove from the heat and squeeze out as much water as you can. Return to the pan and chop with a knife, then leave to cool slightly.

Find your standard Swiss roll tin and wet it under the tap. Drain and lay a piece of baking parchment on top, squashing it into the corners – the damp will help it stick to the tin and lie flat.

Separate the eggs, then when the spinach has cooled slightly add the yolks. Season lightly with salt and pepper plus a pinch of freshly grated nutmeg.

Make the cheese sauce. Melt the butter and stir in the flour in a non-stick pan over a moderate heat, stirring, for about 1 minute. Add the milk using a whisk to avoid lumps and allow to come back to a blip-blop boil. Remove from the heat, add the Gruyère cheese, the crème fraîche, some grated nutmeg and the mustard. Season and stir well.

Now back to the roulade. Whisk the egg whites until you get a firm foam – not stiff peaks as for meringues. Using a metal spoon, fold the egg whites into the spinach mixture until it is all blended, then pour into the Swiss roll tin to a depth of about 1cm (½in). There won't be enough to fill the tin, but don't worry – it won't spread into the corners and will keep its shape. Put on the middle shelf of the oven and bake for about 10 minutes – until it is springy to the touch and just beginning to take colour. It won't rise – don't panic – you are not making a soufflé. Remove from the oven and carefully turn it onto a chopping board, add the filling and flip over before transferring to a serving dish/ plate. Wait a minute or two before peeling off the parchment. Pour on the hot cheese sauce, spreading it with a knife, then carefully roll up the roulade. You need to act quickly so that it is hot when you eat it. Sprinkle on the grated Parmesan and serve with a green salad.

JAN 11TH

Rib-eye steak

INGREDIENTS

- 1 rib-eye steak per person or large enough to share
- 1 garlic clove, crushed
- salt and ground black pepper
- a little vegetable or sunflower oil

Rub the steak with the garlic, salt and a smidgen of oil. If I have time I light up the barbecue but it's easier to heat a griddle pan. There is no need to add any extra oil but heat it well and don't touch the steak until you turn it to seal the other side. It is imperative that the meat rests before slicing it across the grain. Season and serve with fries and a simple green salad made from a butterhead lettuce.

below: *My first attempt at acrylics*

JAN 11TH

Light prawn salad

INGREDIENTS

- 1 standard pack of ready-cooked frozen cold water North Atlantic prawns, shells on
- ½ pack of mixed quinoa and bulgur wheat, cooked according to the pack instructions and left to cool
- ½ green pepper, de-seeded and finely sliced
- 1 small fennel bulb (or ½ large one), finely sliced
- ½ dozen or so cherry tomatoes, cut into quarters
- 1 tbsp freshly mint, chopped
- 1 tbsp fresh parsley, chopped
- 10cm (4in) piece cucumber, cut into small cubes
- 4 spring onions, sliced
- juice of 1 lemon
- salt and ground black pepper
- about 1 tbsp cider or white wine vinegar
- a good splosh of olive oil (about 2 tbsp)

I prefer the flavour and texture of prawns still in their shells, although it is a palaver having to peel them – you can buy them fresh or frozen if you haven't the time nor the inclination. It is very important to remove the dark intestinal vein that runs along the back of the prawns. Once you have prepared them all – about 1½ cups prawns – rinse them well and drain.

Next, put the cooked grains into a bowl and add the prawns, green pepper, fennel, tomatoes, herbs, cucumber, spring onions and lemon juice. Season with salt and pepper and pour the vinegar and olive oil. Mix well and either cover with clingfilm and put aside in the fridge until you are going to eat, or serve straight away. This is a light and very tasty meal – you can always use it to fill toasted pitta breads as a packed lunch for work.

right: *Light prawn salad*

JAN 13TH

I cooked this when we were buried beneath a foot of snow and freezing.

Beef and stout stew

above: *Snowed in*

INGREDIENTS

- 350–450g (12oz–1lb) good stewing steak (I bought a lovely slice of nicely marbled chuck steak the size of a single serving of sirloin for one hungry person. Bulked out with vegetables, this fed four of us without any problem)
- 4 banana shallots, cut into quarters lengthways
- 1 small pack of chestnut mushrooms (about 225g/8oz), sliced
- a sprinkle of mixed herbs, or fresh bay leaf and 2 thyme sprigs
- salt and ground black pepper
- 1 can stout (I had some leftover from having cooked Delia's Christmas puddings last November)
- 1 tsp oil

Preheat the oven to 190°C (170°C fan) mark 5. Trim off any gristly, fatty bits from the meat and cut into cubes about 2.5cm (1in) square.

Heat a flameproof casserole or a large frying pan. Put the oil into the pan and drop in some of the meat, turning it so that it takes on a little colour and the outside is sealed. It is better to do this in a couple of batches so that the pan retains the heat – if you add it all in one go, the heat will reduce rapidly and all you end up with is a grey gloop.

Remove the browned meat from the pan and put to one side, along with the juices. Heat the pan again and add the shallots plus a little water (2 tbsp), stirring every now and again. Cook until the water has evaporated, then add the mushrooms, the browned meat and any juices, the herbs, salt and pepper to taste and about ½ can of the stout. Stir, cover with the lid, bring to the boil (if you are using a frying pan, transfer everything into an ovenproof dish with a lid) and cook in the oven for at least a couple hours. If you have an Aga, use the bottom (simmering) oven. Check every now and again that there is enough liquid, adding more stout or water as necessary although you probably won't have to as the mushrooms will give off a lot of juice. Also, check the meat – you don't want to overcook things and let it disintegrate. This is a very simple stew, and with so few ingredients (note, no garlic this time nor any flour to thicken the gravy) you really taste each individual flavour. Eat it with mashed potatoes and something green, runner beans for example.

JAN 11TH

I check the content of any food I buy and yesterday, for the first time, I bought some venison sausages. They were low in fat, had no artificial additives at all - even the casings were natural. Instead of cooking them like normal bangers I decided to use up a pack of dried Puy lentils.

left: *Mary, my dear little deer*

Venison sausage and Puy lentil casserole

INGREDIENTS

- 3 rashers of very lean smoked streaky bacon or ½ pack of pancetta rashers, chopped
- 1 large onion (red or white) or 2 shallots, chopped
- 1 large carrot, chopped into small cubes
- 1 celery stick, finely chopped
- 2 garlic cloves, crushed
- 2 cups Puy lentils (these are great because they don't need soaking beforehand)
- 2½ cups chicken stock (unsalted if possible)
- 1 good-sized glass of red wine
- 3–4 fresh thyme sprigs, leaves picked or ½ tsp mixed dried herbs
- a good squirt of concentrated tomato purée or concentrated sundried tomato purée (about 1 tbsp)
- salt and ground black pepper
- 1 pack of venison sausages (about 6 sausages)

Preheat the oven to 200°C (180°C fan) mark 6. Heat a flameproof casserole or a large frying pan and put in the bacon or pancetta along with the onion, carrot, celery and garlic. Cook for 5 minutes over a high heat, stirring until the bacon is nearly cooked and the onion is softened. If using a casserole, now add the lentils, stock, wine, herbs, tomato purée, and a few good grinds of pepper. Don't add any salt at this stage or the lentils will remain hard. Bring to the boil, stirring every now and again, then reduce the heat. Either cook on top of the stove on a gentle simmer if you are using a frying pan, or transfer everything into an ovenproof dish with a lid, and cook in the oven. Add more stock, wine or water if the lentils absorb too much liquid (lentils take quite a while to cook and may absorb all the liquid before they are fully cooked).

Seal and brown the sausages in another frying pan (no extra oil), turning them every now and again, for about 5–6 minutes. They don't need to cook, merely take on a bit of colour. Next, remove the pan from the oven and snuggle the sausages into the lentil mixture. Replace the lid and cook very gently in the oven for at least 1½ hours. Check every now and again that there is enough liquid and taste for seasoning.

This can easily be done the day before and the flavours will develop nicely overnight. My chicken stock was not very strong so I added a Knorr chicken stockpot – this is quite salty, so be warned. We had this for supper with some green vegetables but didn't manage to eat all the lentils. We shall have those tonight, reheated thoroughly, with a roast guinea fowl.

JAN 14TH *Instead of cooking a guinea fowl (I forgot to take it out of the freezer) I went shopping and bought a pack of turkey breast steaks instead, which were reduced. Next to them on the shelf was a pack of turkey breast escalopes (also reduced) but they were quite a bit more expensive. I knew that if I put each steak in some clingfilm and bashed it with a rolling pin, I would end up with something similar but cheaper.*

Turkey breast escalopes with creamy sauce

INGREDIENTS

- oil spray
- 1 turkey breast steak per person, bashed and flattened to a few millimetres thick
- a splash of white wine
- about 2 tbsp crème fraîche
- juice of ½ large lemon
- salt and ground black pepper
- fresh parsley, chopped

Heat a frying pan and spray very lightly with oil. Drop in the escalopes and allow to brown. This will only take a minute or two. Turn over and cook for a further minute. Add the white wine, crème fraîche, lemon juice and season with salt and pepper. Swish the pan and stir to mix the sauce. Check that the meat is thoroughly cooked and no pink juices are visible. Remove from the heat, sprinkle with chopped parsley and serve immediately.

You could have this with any sort of rice, pasta or mashed potato and a green veg. Quick, cheap and healthy (you can use half-fat crème fraîche).

top: *A new year, a new dawn*
bottom: *Toby and Suzie with frost on their tails*

Green and pink light salad lunch

INGREDIENTS

1 pack or bunch of fresh asparagus
1 green pepper, deseeded and chopped
1 red onion, chopped
1 celery stick, finely sliced
1 standard jar of chargrilled artichokes, drained and cut into smaller pieces
1 fennel bulb, finely sliced
1 standard pack of smoked salmon slices (or 1 standard can tuna, drained)
juice of 1 lemon
balsamic vinegar
salt and ground black pepper
fresh parsley, chopped

Cook the asparagus until still slightly crunchy. When cool, cut into 2.5cm (1in) slices and mix with the green pepper, onion, celery, artichokes, fennel, smoked salmon or tuna, lemon juice and a dash of balsamic vinegar. There's no need to add more olive oil because of the artichokes, but season with salt and pepper and some chopped parsley.

right: *Green and pink light salad lunch*

JAN 16TH

Quick and easy, low- fat, high-fibre chicken dish

Sweat the onion in a little oil over a moderate heat until soft, then add the frozen vegetables. Stir and add a good cupful or two of chicken stock. Don't cover and cook for 5–8 minutes. Snuggle the chicken breasts among the vegetables and baste with the stock, adding more if necessary. Cover with a lid and simmer gently for about 8–10 minutes, or until the chicken is thoroughly cooked, then check the seasoning. Add the crème fraîche, stir in well and serve immediately sprinkled with chopped parsley or chives. No need for any extra carbs.

INGREDIENTS

1 red onion, sliced
vegetable or sunflower oil
1 cup frozen mixed broad beans, French beans, peas and edamame beans
1–2 cups chicken stock
1 skinless chicken breast per person
salt and ground black pepper
1–2 tbsp crème fraîche
fresh parsley or chives, chopped

below: *Here come the girls*

above: *Aubergines*

JAN 16TH

Sometimes I fancy a meal with no meat but also not the inevitable pasta alternative. These are the vegetables I used – purely what happened to be in the fridge – but you can choose exactly what you fancy, only make sure you have something 'oniony' to give it depth of flavour. It is carb free (unless you have a baked potato like we did) and easy on the tum at night.

Savoury vegetable bake

INGREDIENTS

2 standard bags of spinach
3 leeks, sliced
1 aubergine, cut into slices less than 5mm (¼in) thick
½ head broccoli, cut into florets and then quartered
a handful of cherry tomatoes,
1–2 garlic cloves, chopped
olive oil
½ tsp dried mixed herbs
salt and ground black pepper
2 good cups grated Emmental cheese
½ large tub crème fraîche
2 large eggs

Preheat the oven to 200°C (180°C fan) mark 6. Wash the spinach and place in a pan with no extra water. Stir and cook until it is just beginning to wilt. Remove from the heat, drain and put to one side. Lay the sliced leeks on the bottom of a gratin dish (a rectangular lasagne dish is ideal) and add the sliced aubergine, broccoli, whole cherry tomatoes dotted about and the garlic. Splash on some olive oil and season with the herbs and salt and pepper. Place on the middle shelf of the oven and bake until the vegetables are just about cooked – you may need to drape a piece of foil over it to prevent it burning. This could take about 30 minutes. Remove the dish from the oven, take off the foil and add the wilted spinach, spreading it over the other vegetables.

In a bowl, mix together the cheese, crème fraîche and eggs. Pour this over the vegetables – it will be thick and don't worry if it doesn't quite cover everything, then put back into the oven for a further 10–15 minutes until the top is bubbling and brown.

JAN 18TH

Quick smoked mackerel pâté

Remove and discard the skin from the back of the mackerel fillets and place the fish in a small blender. Add the lemon juice, a few good grinds of black pepper and the rest of the ingredients, except the parsley, and whizz until reasonably smooth but still with texture. Taste and add some salt, if necessary. Put into a small dish and sprinkle with a little chopped parsley. Serve with brown toast or toasted wholemeal pitta breads and a bowl of crispy lettuce (cos) to eat in your fingers. Sometimes I add a few spring onions to add a bit of crunch.

INGREDIENTS

1 standard pack of good-quality smoked mackerel fillets, or smoked trout, or a mixture of both if you find the mackerel too strong a flavour
juice of 1 lemon
salt and ground black pepper
2 heaped tbsp full fat cream cheese
1 heaped tbsp crème fraîche
1 tsp horseradish sauce
fresh parsley, chopped

left: *Freshly caught, freshly dug*

above: *Winter sunlight on bare branches*

JAN 20TH

Fillets of plaice in a parsley sauce with hard-boiled egg

INGREDIENTS

2 whole plaice, as fresh as fresh can be, filleted and skinned by your friendly fishmonger
1–2 eggs, hard-boiled
20g (¾oz) butter
1 tbsp plain flour
about 1 cup milk
salt and ground black pepper
a good handful of fresh parsley, chopped
1 tbsp toasted breadcrumbs

Preheat the oven to 200°C (180°C fan) mark 6. Begin by rinsing the plaice, then pat dry and roll up. Place them, side by side, in a shallow baking dish. Slice the hard-boiled egg(s) and lay over the fish.

Make the white sauce by melting the butter in a non-stick saucepan and stir in the flour. Bring to the boil and stir for a minute or two before whisking in the milk. Bring to the boil again, stirring all the while, until thickened. You may need to add a little more milk. Take off the heat, season with salt and pepper and add the parsley. Pour over the fish, scatter over the breadcrumbs and bake in the oven for about 10 minutes, or until the fish is cooked and the sauce is bubbling.

TIP

Dot with butter to add to the crunch, or even a little grated cheese and lemon zest. Serve with mashed potato and veg of your choice.

Quick vegetable pasta

Cook the spaghetti in a large pan of boiling water (with a pinch of salt added). There is no advantage of adding oil to the water, but make sure it is bubbling furiously before you add the dried pasta, stirring it every now and again to prevent sticking.

Heat a frying pan and add the oil. Add the shallot, stir and simmer for 5 minutes. Add the sliced mushroom, stir, then cover the pan with a loose-fitting lid. After 2–3 minutes, stir in the tomatoes, garlic, herbs, salt and pepper. Cover and simmer for 5–6 minutes until cooked. Add the crème fraîche and mix well. Remove from the heat and put to one side.

When the pasta is cooked (according to the pack – *al dente*, with a little bite), drain quickly (reserving some of the water) and return to the pan with a small amount of the cooking liquid.

Add the vegetable mixture and stir well, then transfer to warmed bowls. Sprinkle with grated Parmesan cheese and serve immediately.

INGREDIENTS

enough dried spaghetti for 2
salt and ground black pepper
1 tbsp olive oil
1 shallot, chopped
1 large open mushroom, sliced
a handful of cherry tomatoes, chopped
1 garlic clove, chopped
a good sprinkle of dried Italian mixed herbs
1 tbsp fresh basil and parsley, torn or roughly chopped
salt and ground black pepper
1 heaped tbsp crème fraîche
freshly grated Parmesan cheese

above: *Chilli eggs*

JAN 23RD

A delicious, filling but light and healthy start to the day.

Chilli eggs

INGREDIENTS

For one you will need:

1 small red onion, very finely chopped
as many small, sweet cherry tomatoes as you fancy, cut into small pieces
1 fresh red or green chilli, deseeded, the inner white ribs removed and very finely chopped
1–2 eggs
salt and ground black pepper
fresh coriander leaves
1 small ripe avocado or ½ large one, peeled, stoned and sliced
½ lime to squeeze over the avocado

Heat a small non-stick frying pan (an omelette pan for example) and add a splash of water. Add the chopped onion, stir and allow to cook gently until the water has evaporated, about 5 minutes. By using water instead of oil, the onion will cook and be devoid of extra calories. Add the chopped tomatoes and as much chilli as you want, stir and cook over a moderate heat until they are soft. Move the vegetables to the edge of the pan, making a space, then drop in an egg – two if you are very peckish. Season with salt and pepper and swizzle until the egg is cooked: you are aiming at a cross between scrambled eggs and a sort of rustic omelette. Tip on to a plate, sprinkle with coriander leaves and serve immediately with the avocado, sprinkled with lime juice.
I like this with fizzy water and Ryvita.

JAN 24TH

Yet another of my great-great grandmother's recipes.

Simply the best orange marmalade

INGREDIENTS

1.3kg (3lb) Seville oranges (these are the bitter oranges that only available at the beginning of the year)

2.2kg (5lb) granulated sugar (put into an ovenproof bowl and warmed in the oven)

Place a small metal dish or saucer in the icebox or freezer to chill. Wash the oranges, concentrating on the area where the stalk was and place them whole in a large pan. Cover the fruit with cold water, bring to the boil, then reduce the heat and simmer gently until the skin is so soft it can be pierced with the head of a pin. Remove the fruit and measure out 700ml (1¼ pints) of the cooking liquid, discard the remainder.

One by one, cut the fruit in half, removing the pips as you go into a small dish. Chop or slice the orange skin as finely as you wish. Put the reserved orange water into a large preserving pan and add the warmed sugar. Bring to the boil and cook for 5–10 minutes, watching very carefully as the syrup could easily boil over – it will as soon as you turn your back on it, believe me. Put the pips into a small piece of muslin and secure well. Add this plus the chopped oranges to the sugar syrup, stir and bring back to the boil. Cook until the orange pith has become transparent. This could take quite a while, over 20 minutes, skimming off any scum as it appears. Stir frequently to prevent burning and sticking. When setting point is reached, using a jam funnel, carefully fill hot sterilised jam jars (see page 5) and seal immediately.

Sometimes I vary the sugar and instead of using 100 per cent white granulated, I ring the changes with a mixture of muscovado, demerara or golden granulated – it is a matter of taste. The muscovado has a deep, rich and intense flavour – a bit too treacly for me on its own – but a small amount added to white sugar does darken the colour of the marmalade. You can also add a splosh of whisky 5 minutes before the end. Adults only.

above: *Marmalade in the making*
below: *Chunky marmalade*

JAN 26TH *I love orchids but I have never had (until now that is) any success in keeping them going after they have finished flowering. I bought a beautiful specimen before Christmas over a year ago and it continued flowering well into March. It looked healthy, giving it the minimum of care with an occasional splash of rainwater and no plant food until one day I noticed the beginnings of a bud. This is the result and if anything, the flowers are even larger than last year's. So, don't throw away your orchids – neglect them and you should be rewarded.*

above: *Orchid – or an angel?*
below: *Out on day release*

JAN 29TH *I let the chickens out again this morning to scratch around as they had such fun the other day. I went shopping and when I came back, four fluffy, clucky little girls came racing across the lawn to greet me. Somehow, they had found their way around the field into the garden. I left them to play in the flower beds and it was a joy to watch. Roll on tomorrow's eggs.*

Aubergine bake

Preheat the oven to 200°C (180°C fan) mark 6. Begin by heating a griddle pan if you have one – if not, use a solid based frying pan. Spray with a little oil and add as many slices of aubergine as can sit side by side in the pan. Brown for 2–3 minutes, don't add further oil but turn the aubergines over and brown for another minute. Remove and put to one side. Add another spray of oil and cook the remaining aubergine slices.

Next, heat a little olive oil in the pan, add the shallots or onions and about 1 cup water. Bring to the boil, then reduce the heat and simmer until the liquid has evaporated, stirring every now and again. Add the mushrooms and garlic, stir and cook for a further 3 minutes.

Layer the base of a medium-sized gratin (lasagne type) dish with some of the aubergine slices, sprinkle over half the shallot and mushroom mixture and dot with half the cherry tomatoes. Add the slices of one of the mozzarella balls, a sprinkle of herbs, half the can of tomatoes and season with salt and pepper. Lay the remaining aubergine slices (it doesn't matter if they overlap) on top, then the remaining ingredients in the same order as above. Drizzle over about ½ cup olive oil, then either cover with clingfilm and put to one side to cook later, or bake in the oven for about 30 minutes until the vegetables are almost cooked through.

In a bowl, beat the egg with the crème fraîche and add the grated cheese. Spread this over the vegetables, sprinkle with a little more grated cheese – and if you like a crunch, sprinkle the breadcrumbs over the top. Return to the oven for a further 10 minutes or so, or until the top is bubbling and golden brown, and the crumbs crisp. Eat on its own or as a single accompaniment to any sort of lamb or chicken.

INGREDIENTS

oil spray
1 large aubergine, cut into 5mm (¼in) thick slices
olive oil
4 shallots or 3 small red or white onions, sliced
½–¾ punnet of small (but not tiny button) mushrooms, roughly sliced or quartered
1–2 garlic cloves, chopped (the green mid-rib removed)
dozen or so cherry tomatoes, cut in half
2 low fat mozzarella balls, sliced
fresh herbs, such as basil, parsley or oregano or a good sprinkling of dried Italian herbs
400g (14oz) can chopped tomatoes
salt and ground black pepper
1 large egg
½ large tub crème fraîche
1–2 cups grated Gruyère cheese (Emmental can go a bit stringy, too much Cheddar and it becomes greasy), plus extra to sprinkle
2 slices wholemeal bread, whizzed into crumbs, if you like

JAN 30TH

I bought a pack of Barley Mixture grains by Pedon and once cooked, instantly cooled and mixed with other bits and pieces, they made a perfect, nutty, delicious and extremely healthy salad. Quinoa or any other grain will also be suitable.

Nutty salad

INGREDIENTS

- 1 standard pack of Pedon dried barley mixture grains (low in fat, extremely high in fibre and a thoroughly good addition to your diet)
- 1 celery stick, finely sliced
- 10 cherry tomatoes, cut into quarters
- 15cm (6in) piece cucumber, chopped into small cubes
- a handful of fresh parsley and mint, roughly chopped
- 6 spring onions, chopped
- either cooked (cold leftover) ham, chicken, hard-boiled eggs, tuna, prawns, whatever you like
- juice of 1 lemon
- a good splash of vinegar (use whatever you like)
- a good drizzle of olive oil
- salt and ground black pepper

Cook the grains according to the pack instructions and add a further 10 minutes' cooking time. Drain, rinse under the cold tap and either soak quickly in cold water and drain again, or allow to cool naturally, depending on how quickly you need to use them.

Add the celery, cherry tomatoes, cucumber, herbs and the spring onions to a salad bowl with your chosen protein. I had boiled a piece of smoked gammon and had a chunk left over, which I de-fatted and cut into small pieces and added these to the mix.

Pile on the cold grains plus the lemon juice, vinegar and olive oil, seasoning with salt and pepper. Stir well and it's ready to serve. It's really, really, really nice – all on its own, or (as my darling husband did) with the added accompaniment of a dollop of good mayonnaise.

JAN 31ST

While shopping this morning I spotted a pack of special pasta flour. Into the trolley it went along with a vow to dig out my pasta machine once back home. Miracle of miracles, I found it half hidden and gathering dust beneath my electric lean machine griller – as good a place as any. If you don't have the time or the patience, any fresh or dried pasta fits the bill.

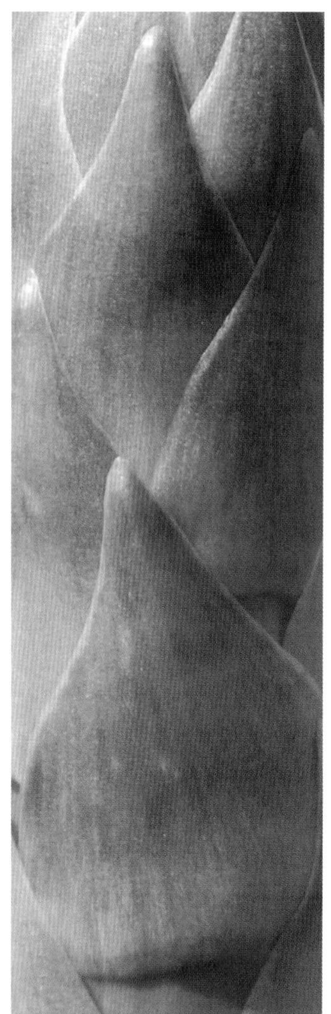

Asparagus pasta

INGREDIENTS

300g (10½oz) pasta flour
3 large eggs, beaten
a pinch of salt

FOR THE SAUCE

1 large bunch of asparagus, cut diagonally (it's prettier) into 2.5cm (1in) pieces
salt and ground black pepper
½ tub of ricotta cheese
½ tub crème fraîche
olive oil
fresh basil leaves, torn
freshly grated Parmesan cheese

To make the pasta I tipped the flour, eggs and salt into the food processor and within minutes had a lovely elastic dough, wrapped it in clingfilm and left it to chill in the fridge for 30 minutes. As I was up against time, my accompaniment to the pasta had to be ultra-quick to prepare. I boiled the asparagus in a little salty water until it was just about cooked but still with a bit of bite. In a bowl, I mixed the ricotta, crème fraîche, a splash of olive oil, salt and pepper and a few torn basil leaves.

I made tagliatelle in the machine, which was easy once I realised you have to keep everything lightly floured or it will stick together. I dropped the lot into the pan of salty boiling water. I am not of the brigade, which eats pasta almost raw; I like it to be firm but not white and hard in the middle. The pasta drained, I tipped it back into the pan and added the other ingredients. Tossed well, served up in warmed bowls and dusted with a liberal amount of Parmesan it made a splendid lunch – and I had made everything from scratch. *Molto bene.*

above: *Up close and personal*

top: *Gnome place like gnome*
bottom: *From the kitchen window*

FEB 1ST *I ventured out in the rain with my camera in the hope of cheering myself up on a miserable day. There are definitely signs of spring: the birds were 'twitterpating' (my mother's expression) and even a fledgling great tit was feeding himself with gusto – unheard of at this time of the year. Roll on March.*

With a glimmer (albeit watery) of sunshine and no ice on the car windscreen I feel that the worst of the winter is now behind us. As I have done over the past week, I let out the chickens so that they could roam free in the field and the garden and immediately they headed for the terrace. They amused themselves for hours hoovering up the bird seed kicked out by the blue tits who were telling me quite clearly that they didn't like the mixed food I bought yesterday and preferred sunflower hearts. The chickens didn't mind and did a great job of eating everything on the ground until they discovered the small pansies in the tubs, devouring the young leaves with the mannerisms of a dowager duchess taking her young nephew to tea at the Ritz.

I gave up on the ironing to stand and look out of the kitchen window. The garden had become a safari park: in no time at all I spotted seven blackbirds, already pairing up, too many goldfinches to count, dozens of blue and great tits, sparrows, a little Billy-no-mates-solitary wagtail, two squirrels, a greater spotted woodpecker followed by a thrush, greenfinches, chaffinches, pigeons as fat and as solidly built as our near defunct battleships cruising up the lawn in formation, a Jenny wren scuttling from underneath a large terracotta tub, robins, a yellowhammer and a nuthatch who was struggling to get at the remaining peanuts. In among all this band of featherhood wandered our five girls, clucking, chattering and nibbling at anything to hand. I could watch them for hours.

For a pleasant change from chicken I opted to thaw four free-range quail I had in the freezer. When they were thoroughly defrosted I cut away the elastic truss and then removed the tiny, brittle wishbones from each bird. It is a bit fiddly to do, but if you have a sharp, pointed knife you can winkle around the bone and then either cut or pull it out in one go. It will probably snap so make sure you remove any remaining shards.

above: *Five go out to play*

Quail with grapes

INGREDIENTS

1 tbsp olive oil
1 medium-large shallot, chopped
1 garlic clove, crushed
4 quail
1–2 tbsp brandy or Calvados
115–175g (4–6oz) green, seedless grapes, halved (if you manage to find a shop selling muscat grapes – in season for a brief period – March to May – they will add a unique flavour to the dish)
200ml (7fl oz) chicken stock
salt and ground black pepper

Preheat the oven to 200°C (180°C fan) mark 6. Begin by heating the olive oil in a flameproof casserole and add the chopped shallot and garlic, plus a good splash of water. Stir every few moments and by the time the water has evaporated the shallot will have softened. Add the whole birds and brown briefly on each side. Spoon on the brandy or Calvados and carefully ignite it with a match – this will burn off the alcohol but leave the flavour. Surround the birds with the grapes, then add the chicken stock and gently season with salt and pepper. If you use a concentrated chicken stock cube or liquid it will be very salty in its undiluted state so before adding it to the casserole, mix with water in a jug and then add the required amount to the dish. Use the leftover stock for soup. Cover with the lid and either simmer very gently on the top of the stove or cook in the oven for about 20–30 minutes until the birds are cooked through and there are no pink juices.

You can either serve the quail whole or, for fussy eaters, you can carefully lift off the breast meat and cut away the legs and thighs and serve only these pieces on the bone. They are definitely best eaten with your fingers. Creamy, fluffy mashed potato marries perfectly with the tangy juices and any green vegetable of your choice.

FEB 6TH

Lately we have been enjoying visits from friends for lunch rather than for an evening meal and fish is the ideal dish. It is light, quick to prepare and cook, one favourite being John Dory. It is a firm, meaty, very white fish and fillets beautifully, one fillet being sufficient for one serving. It's not cheap, but there are no fiddly bones which can spoil the pleasure. As an accompaniment, I make a very easy butter sauce. Simon had unfortunately sold out of John Dory so I chose two beautiful bream caught off the shore at Brighton, which he kindly filleted for me.

Butter sauce for fish

INGREDIENTS

1 shallot, very finely chopped
1 glass of white wine, Vermouth or Noilly Prat
1 tbsp white wine vinegar
55g (2oz) butter (unsalted if you have it)
1 cup double cream
salt and ground black pepper

Put the shallot, wine and vinegar into a small saucepan and bubble away until most of the liquid has evaporated then, little by little, stir or whisk in the butter. Add the cream and bring back to the boil. Taste and adjust the seasoning and, if you want a smooth sauce, sieve it then pour it into a warm jug.

Simple fried fish with egg sauce

INGREDIENTS

sunflower or vegetable oil
3 tbsp plain flour to dust
finely grated zest of 1 lemon
salt and ground black pepper
enough fillets of fish – your choice: haddock, cod, pollock etc, for 4
a knob of butter

Heat the oil in a large frying pan. In the meantime, have a dish in which you have put the flour. Add the lemon zest, season well with salt and pepper and mix. Pat the fish dry with kitchen paper and coat with the seasoned flour. Lay gently in the hot (not smoking) oil and when all the fillets are in the frying pan (if you are cooking quite a few fillets you may need to have two pans on the go), add the butter for flavour and baste the fish. It will cook extremely quickly so turn it after a minute to cook the other side. Serve immediately with the grated lemon cut into four and with steamed potatoes over which you have sprinkled some chopped parsley and the egg sauce below.

Egg sauce

INGREDIENTS

30g (1oz) butter
30g (1oz) plain flour
1¼ cups milk
4 eggs, hard-boiled peeled and finely chopped
salt and ground black pepper

This is so easy and simple to make. It is silky, velvety and goes extremely well with fried fish. I made a white sauce by melting the butter in a pan and stirring in the flour. When bubbling I carefully stirred or whisked in the milk and let it come to the boil, stirring all the while to prevent lumps. I cooked this for a minute, then added the chopped eggs and seasoned well with salt and pepper. I kept it warm and served in a dish with a small ladle. It needs to be thick but not solid.

above: *Blowing away the cobwebs*

FEB 7TH

I know it might sound daft to be excited by such simple things but I hung out the washing to dry in the garden for the first time this year. Bliss. Domestic goddess I am not but, with careful folding, I won't have to iron ANYTHING.

Pan-fried savoury sweet potato

INGREDIENTS

vegetable or sunflower oil
1 sweet potato, peeled and spiralised or grated
1 red onion, sliced
1 large carrot, grated
salt and ground black pepper

Heat a very small dash of oil in a non-stick frying pan (omelette-sized) and pile in the vegetables. Stir-fry over a moderate heat until cooked. Season. Serve with a roughly mashed ripe avocado to which you have added some lime juice (preferably) but I only had lemon. Drizzle with sweet chilli jam or mango chutney.

FEB 15TH *I experimented this week making small fruit 'souffles' without flour, using ground almonds instead. It didn't quite work out as I had hoped partly because I rushed things and hadn't mixed the egg yolk properly with the almonds, and once cooked there were a few lumps. In spite of this it did taste really good and for Valentine's night I made them again, but with a few adjustments. This amount makes four individual puds.*

Flourless fruit surprises

First, stew the fruit on a gentle heat with enough sugar to taste. Don't boil but bring to a simmer, then remove from the heat when the juices have begun to run. Leave to cool and then pass through a sieve. You want to end up with about 300ml (½ pint) of purée.

Just before you are ready to have your pudding, preheat the oven to 220°C (200°C fan) mark 7 and boil a kettle of water. Next, separate the egg yolks from the whites. Blend the yolks with the fruit purée using a fork or small hand whisk. Add the ground almonds and a little more (1 heaped tsp) sugar. Make sure the bowl in which you are going to whisk the egg whites is squeaky clean and whisk until they are firm but not too stiff – you want soft peaks.

Add the chocolate chips to the fruit purée and fold in the whisked egg whites. Pour into small individual ramekins, about 10cm (4in) in diameter and 7cm (2¾in) high, three-quarters of the way up. Put them into a small baking dish half-filled with boiling water. Place in the centre of the oven for about 10–15 minutes, but check after 10 minutes to see how they are getting on – don't be scared, just open the oven door slowly to avoid a sudden draught. You want them to have risen and for the top to have taken on a little colour. When cooked, remove from the oven, carefully lift them on to a cold plate and dust the soufflés with a little icing sugar, then serve immediately. As it was Valentine's night, I decorated mine with a heart.

above: *Flourless fruit suprises*

INGREDIENTS

- about 280g (10oz) frozen red fruits, such as raspberries, blackberries, redcurrants, blueberries, etc. or a mixture of several (whatever tickles your fancy)
- caster sugar to taste
- 2 eggs
- 50g (1¾oz) ground almonds
- 1 heaped tbsp dark chocolate chips (found in the baking section)

UPDATE

They certainly worked better than at the first attempt and the flavour of the chocolate worked well with the fruit: they weren't too sweet but, be warned, they sink as soon as they come out of the oven, however this didn't affect the taste. I am going to ring the changes with puréed apricots, plums, rhubarb or peaches adding vanilla extract or seeds. I might also switch the ground almonds for fresh white breadcrumbs but won't necessarily include the chocolate chips.

Still thinking in terms of low fat/low carbs (but not no fat/no carbs) this is a tasty, filling and quick meal.

Breaded turkey escalopes

INGREDIENTS

2 large turkey breast steaks (cheaper than veal)
finely grated zest of 1 lemon (cut into 4 pieces afterwards and served with the cooked turkey)
4 slices wholemeal bread, blitzed to a fine crumb in the blender
1 tbsp finely grated Parmesan cheese, if you like
2 heaped tbsp plain flour
1 large egg, beaten
olive oil to cook
dried pasta of your choice (I used spaghetti)

FOR THE TOMATO SAUCE

⅓ cup olive oil
3–4 garlic cloves, crushed
225g (8oz) tomatoes, roughly chopped
salt and ground black pepper
½ tsp granulated sugar

Begin by stretching a piece of clingfilm on to your work surface. Lay on one of the turkey steaks and either fold over the clingfilm or stretch another piece on top. Bash the meat with a rolling pin until it is much thinner, rolling it out as well until you are happy with the thickness: less than 5mm (¼in). Cut into two (or more if you wish) and remove any white stringy bits.

You can prepare this part in advance. Begin by mixing the lemon zest into the breadcrumbs. You can also add finely grated Parmesan, if you like. Next, dip each piece of turkey breast into the flour, then coat them in the beaten egg and then into the lemony breadcrumbs. Lay them (not touching) on a plate and leave in the fridge until you are ready to cook them.

To make the tomato sauce, heat the olive oil in a saucepan, add the garlic and stir. After a few moments, add the tomatoes, a pinch of salt, a good grinding of black pepper and the sugar. Simmer for 10–15 minutes until it has reduced and is slightly jammy. This also can be prepared in advance and is the easiest, quickest sauce for any sort of pasta to be served as a meal on its own plus shredded basil and lots of grated Parmesan or pecorino cheese.

Preheat the oven to 200°C (180°C fan) mark 6. Before cooking the pasta, put the turkey pieces on to a heated baking tray and drizzle (or spray) with a little olive oil. Place on the middle shelf of the oven and bake for about 20 minutes, or less, depending on the thickness of the escalopes, until they are nicely browned and crispy. Make sure there are no runny pink juices.

Cook the spaghetti in a large pan of salted boiling water until *al dente* – there is no advantage of adding oil to the water, but make sure it is bubbling furiously before you add the dried pasta, stirring it every now and again to prevent sticking. Drain quickly and, with some of the cooking water still attached to the pasta, tip it back into the pan and keep warm. Serve topped with some of the tomato sauce, alongside the crispy turkey escalopes and the lemon into wedges.

FEB 17TH *Looking through the kitchen window this morning at around 8 o'clock there, before my eyes, were our two faithful, old friends. They are wild mallards who have been honouring us with their presence every spring for years. The first time they landed on the lawn was much later in March. Ma said that we ought to name them and, since Gwyneth Paltrow had just won an Oscar they were christened Gwyneth and Oscar Poultry. They have had chicks under the artichoke plants, on the flat roof of the cottage, under the ivy (snuggled against a wall) in an enclosed courtyard and heaven knows where else. They are absolutely devoted to each other and while Gwyneth fills her boots on corn on the terrace, Oscar stands to one side patiently and, only when she scuttles off to the pond, does he allow himself a bite. I wonder where they will make their nest this year?*

above: *Cyclamen coum*
left: *Two old friends return to the fold*

FEB 19TH

Smoked trout mousse

INGREDIENTS

1 pack of smoked trout
1 fresh rainbow trout
1 tsp Dijon mustard
1 tbsp good-quality mayonnaise
1tbsp crème fraîche
1 tbsp cream cheese
1 tsp horseradish cream
juice of ½ lemon
salt and ground black pepper

Line a small ramekin (3–4in in diameter) with some clingfilm and then with the strips of smoked trout, which is cheaper and less oily than smoked salmon. Put the rainbow trout in a shallow pan with enough plain water almost to cover the fish, cover with a lid, bring to the boil and poach for about 5 minutes. Remove the fish carefully, peel off the skin and cut away the fillets, making sure there are no bones. This takes time but it is essential. When completely cold, blitz the fish quickly in a small food processor with the mustard, mayonnaise, crème fraîche, cream cheese, horseradish cream, lemon juice and salt and pepper. Pour the mixture into the ramekin, fold over any smoked trout lining the ramekin and chill for at least 2 hours, overnight if possible. Turn out on to a pretty plate and serve with some crispy lettuce, rocket, lemon wedges and cherry tomatoes. To add extra piquancy and bite, dust with a little cayenne pepper.

right: *Smoked trout mousse*

FEB 21ST

Sweet peppers stuffed with quinoa and feta

Preheat the oven to 200°C (180°C fan) mark 6. Mix the quinoa with the chives, parsley, garlic, lemon zest and juice and crumbled feta cheese. Season to taste. Cut the peppers in half, remove the seeds and any of the white rib then fill with the quinoa. Drizzle with olive oil and bake in the oven until cooked, about 30–40 minutes. Serve at room temperature.

INGREDIENTS

1 standard pouch of cooked quinoa
fresh chives, chopped
fresh parsley, chopped
1 garlic clove, crushed
finely grated zest and juice of 1 lemon
about 1 tbsp feta cheese, crumbled
different coloured sweet peppers, one per person if small, half if large
salt and ground black pepper
olive oil

left: *Sweet peppers stuffed with quinoa and feta*

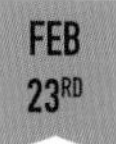

Roast poussin

INGREDIENTS

1 poussin (for 2 people or if for 1, keep the other half to eat cold with salad the next day)
2 heaped tsp hot paprika
2 tsp dried mixed herbs
juice of ½ lemon
salt and ground black pepper
1 garlic clove, crushed
olive oil

Preheat the oven to 200°C (180°C fan) mark 6. Begin by removing the trussing string from the poussin. Put the paprika into a small bowl, add the dried mixed herbs, lemon juice, salt and pepper to taste and the garlic and mix well. Rub this all over the poussin. Place the poussin in a shallow roasting dish, drizzle (or spray as I did) with a little olive oil and roast on the middle shelf of the oven for about 30 minutes, or until the juices run clear. Baste it once or twice if you remember to during cooking. When done, leave to rest for a few minutes, then drain off any fat and cut the bird into quarters. Serve with the cooking juices, chips and a green salad. This is also great picnic food if served cold with lots of nibbly bits to chew on, eating it with your fingers.

below: *Fabulous forced rhubarb*

FEB 23RD

A cause for celebration! About a month ago I placed our old terracotta forcing pots over the rhubarb plants and forgot about them. This morning, on my way back from the chickens, I took a peak and to my delight there was a mass of beautiful, pink fleshy stalks growing. The photograph shows this heavenly harvest, sitting on our old wrought-iron bench which we have just recently had re-sprayed a deep cherry pink – much to my brother's horror. I have yet to convince him that this 'statement' colour will look gorgeous with tulips in the spring and with geraniums later on.

Stewed rhubarb

above: *Stewed rhubarb and strawberries*

INGREDIENTS

6 stalks forced rhubarb
4oz frozen strawberries
juice of 1 orange
caster or golden granulated sugar to taste

I always have frozen strawberries in the freezer and I love cooking them with rhubarb; they add a natural sweetness, which means I can cut down on sugar. Wash the rhubarb stalks thoroughly (slugs love the warm, dark confines of the forcing pot) and trim off the bright leaves and the slippery root ends. DON'T be tempted to eat the pretty leaves – they are poisonous and must be removed and discarded. Using scissors, cut the stalks into 2.5cm (1in) lengths and put in a shallow pan with the frozen strawberries. Add the orange juice, then bring it gently to simmering point and stir carefully – you don't want to break up the fruit. When the rhubarb is soft enough to be pierced with a knife, remove from the heat and allow to cool. Serve with egg custard below – what could be a better harbinger of spring?

Egg custard

INGREDIENTS

1 heaped tbsp caster sugar
2½ cups milk (full fat makes it richer) plus extra
1 tsp vanilla extract
1 egg yolk, plus 1 whole egg
1 heaped tsp cornflour

Bring the sugar, milk and vanilla to boiling point in a pan – this is called 'scalding'. Beat the eggs in a small heatproof bowl and whisk in the cornflour plus a little extra COLD milk. When the milk and sugar are hot, remove from the heat and pour a little into the egg mixture, whisking well. Continue adding a little more of the milk and then, using a fine sieve (to remove any stringy bits of egg and remaining lumps), carefully pour the egg mixture into the remaining warm milk. Gently bring back to boiling point stirring or whisking all the while so that the eggs don't scramble. As soon as it begins to thicken, remove from the heat and pour into a bowl to cool, and chill before serving.

FEB 26TH

Last night I roasted a piece of pork. It was an odd cut: not quite spare ribs, not quite a normal roast, next to the belly but lean and extremely tender. There was some left over and I remembered, in the long distant past having had a dish of macaroni which included minced pork, at a golf club in Southern Spain. Here is what I did with the leftovers.

Interesting pasta bake

INGREDIENTS

leftover cold pork
dried pasta of your choice (macaroni or spirals are a good choice)
1 leek, finely sliced
olive oil
1 small shallot, finely sliced
½ tub crème fraîche
1 tsp dried Italian herbs
salt and ground black pepper
olive oil
1 cup grated Emmental or Gruyère cheese
2 slices brown bread, crumbled

Preheat the oven to 200°C (180°C fan) mark 6. I took all the meat (discarding any fat) from the bones and quickly whizzed it in the food processor but not too much, as I didn't want to pulverise it into a paste. While the pasta was cooking I sweated the leek and shallot in a small pan in a bit of oil over a moderate heat until soft. In another small bowl, I mixed the crème fraîche, herbs and some salt and pepper together.

When the pasta was *al dente*, I drained it (retaining a little of the cooking water), put it back in the pan and added the cheese, the creamy herb mixture, the leek and shallot and the minced cooked pork and tipped it into a shallow ovenproof dish sprinkling the brown breadcrumbs on top for a bit of crunch. I baked it in the oven for about 15 minutes until it was really piping hot and brown on top.

FEB 28TH

Baked rhubarb custard

INGREDIENTS

450g (1lb) forced fresh rhubarb
1 large egg
1 tbsp plain flour
150ml (¼ pint) single cream
caster sugar to taste

Preheat the oven to 200°C (180°C fan) mark 6. Wash the rhubarb stalks thoroughly and trim off the bright leaves and the slippery root ends. DON'T eat the leaves – remember they are poisonous. Using scissors, cut the stalks into 2.5cm (1in) pieces and put into a shallow ovenproof dish.

In a bowl, mix the egg, flour, cream and sugar together and pour over the raw fruit. Bake on the middle shelf of the oven until it is just beginning to take on a bit of colour, about 20 minutes or so. This is best served at room temperature with an extra sprinkling of caster sugar scattered on top, and a dollop of whipped double cream.

TIP

You could always add a few sliced strawberries, freshly grated nutmeg or vanilla to the rhubarb.

left: *Ouch!*

SPRING

above: *First sign of Spring*

Easy peasy marinade for just about everything

INGREDIENTS

A good slug of mushroom ketchup (a storecupboard 'must')
juice of 1 lemon (plus a little of the zest if you are using it for chicken)
soy sauce
1–2 garlic cloves, crushed (no need to peel first)
1 tsp Worcestershire sauce
ground black pepper

Mix everything together well, add the meat, steaks or drumsticks, making sure everything is covered. Seal with clingfilm and put in the fridge for at least 1 hour.

TIP

You can add some chilli flakes if you want extra heat, or paprika (hot or smoked), fresh or dried herbs – I add chopped rosemary if I'm cooking lamb, sage for pork, thyme and tarragon for chicken or beef.

Dear Elizabeth,

Thank you so much for contacting me via my blog. Your generous, kind and encouraging comments made me cry. I am so glad you are enjoying reading about my antics and for taking the time to contact me. Hopefully you will also enjoy dipping into A Compost Kind of Girl *when it arrives. Good luck with the chickens. Remember, if you want eggs, get hard-working, affectionate and tame ISA Warrens (little brown biddies) or similar types - the breeder will recommend the ideal chickens for you. The more well-bred, privately educated the feathered friend, generally fewer eggs are laid - they sacrifice production for beauty.*

With kindest regards,
Bryony

MAR 4TH *The little snippets of growing salads I bought from the supermarket some months ago and planted in the greenhouse have done really well. In spite of the very cold spell in February they are now big enough to pick several good-sized leaves from each lettuce. Apart from that, I have done no gardening at all for weeks except to make a start on pruning the roses. This takes quite a while as we have dozens of them ranging from a tangle of ramblers to climbing varieties on the trellis and a load of shrub roses. It's worth taking a bit of trouble as you reap the rewards in June. One thing I am very bad at is feeding them – maybe this year will be different.*

The shepherd's hut is coming back to life after the bleakness of deep winter and the daffodils are beginning to flower around it in the meadow. If the sun shines this week I shall venture down with a large mug of coffee and gaze dreamily at the countryside and fields.

above: *I can tolerate this little fellow in my vegetable patch*
below: *Suzie on springtime walkabout*

I made this heart-warming soup, having cooked a small piece of smoked gammon last night. I always boil ham with a few onions, carrots, stick or two of celery, leeks if I have them, parsley ditto and a few grinds of pepper. I don't add any salt because sometimes (usually in fact) the ham is salty enough. Don't throw away the stock – it makes wonderful soup.

Pea and mint soup

INGREDIENTS

- 2½ cups ham stock (see page 67)
- 1 large potato, peeled and chopped
- 2 cups frozen peas (or 225g/8oz fresh if available)
- 1 tbsp fresh mint leaves, chopped
- 1¼ cups milk
- ground black pepper

Put the stock in a saucepan with the potato and peas. Bring to the boil, then reduce the heat and simmer until the potatoes are soft, about 10 minutes. Add the mint leaves and milk, then blitz with a hand-held blender and taste for seasoning.

TIP

A plain soup with just potatoes and a couple of cloves of garlic added to the stock is another option. Alternatively, try carrots and the juice of a large orange... or some fresh coriander leaves... or leeks and more potatoes.

right: *Straight from the pod*

MAR 9TH

Fishcakes with a difference

Poach the fish in the milk with the butter, pepper and bay leaf. This will only take about 5 minutes. Lift the fish from the pan on to a plate, take off the skin and remove any stray bones. Flake the fish into small pieces and allow to cool.

In the meantime, steam the potatoes in their skins, then drain and crush.

When the fish is cool enough to handle, mix the flaked fish, potatoes, watercress and lemon zest together. Add more pepper and pinch of salt, then form the mixture into four cakes. Place the gram flour in a bowl, beat the egg in another bowl and put the breadcrumbs in a third bowl. Roll each fishcake in the gram flour, then dip in the beaten egg and roll in Panko crumbs until coated. Leave to chill in the fridge for at least 15 minutes in order to settle.

Heat enough oil for shallow-frying in a frying pan over a moderate heat and fry the cakes for about 2–3 minutes on each side until golden brown. For a lighter touch, spray with low calorie oil and bake in an oven preheated to 200°C (180°C fan) mark 6 until golden brown and piping hot.

INGREDIENTS

- A piece of undyed, smoked haddock
- a little milk
- 15g (½oz) butter
- ground black pepper
- 1 bay leaf
- 6 small new potatoes, skins on
- 1 standard bag or bunch of watercress, chopped
- finely grated zest of 1 lemon
- salt
- enough gram (chickpea) flour to coat
- 1 egg, beaten
- enough Panko breadcrumbs to coat
- vegetable or sunflower oil

MAR 10TH

Two friends came to supper. We cooked the main course and, as it was Pancake Day, they offered to do the pudding. Deal. The pancakes were filled with sliced banana, chocolate sprinkles and Aunt Jemima's syrup all the way from the good ole US of A. There was a small amount of batter left after our feasting and popped in the fridge overnight, it still looked pretty reasonable the next day. Waste not, want not is my motto (enhanced by the beginning of Lent) and so I used it for our lunch. The recipe overleaf is pretty basic but we enjoyed it and sometimes simple is good.

below: *Herring on a red plate*

above: *Baby spinach*

Spinach and ricotta pancakes with a cheesy sauce

INGREDIENTS FOR 2 PEOPLE

- 300ml (½ pint) pancake batter (your own favourite recipe or buy some instant) or ready-made pancakes
- 1 standard pack of baby spinach
- 1 standard tub of ricotta cheese
- salt and ground black pepper
- ¼ tsp freshly grated nutmeg

FOR THE CHEESE SAUCE

- 30g (1oz) butter
- 1 tbsp plain flour
- 150ml (¼ pint) milk, plus extra if the sauce is too thick
- 1 tsp Dijon mustard
- 2–3 tbsp grated cheese, such as Emmental, Gruyère or Cheddar
- freshly grated Parmesan cheese to top

The pancakes can be prepared in advance and kept to one side, ready to fill later. Wash the spinach thoroughly, drain and cook in a pan with no added water, stirring and squashing down until it is much reduced, therefore cooked enough. Tip into a sieve and remove as much of the water as possible.

Put the drained spinach into a bowl, then add the ricotta cheese, a few grinds of black pepper, a little salt and grated nutmeg and mix well.

For the cheese sauce, in a non-stick pan, melt the butter and stir in the flour, then stir until it boils. Quickly add the milk, stirring or whisking as you go to avoid lumps, then allow to come to the boil, stirring all the time. Once it bubbles, remove from the heat, stir in the mustard and the grated cheese.

Preheat the oven to 200°C (180°C fan) mark 6. Taking each pancake, one at a time, lay it flat and spoon on some of the spinach mixture down the middle, in a line, about 1 tbsp. Fold over the pancake into a sausage and put into a shallow, baking dish. Continue until you have used up all the spinach stuff. These should lie in the dish side by side, like sardines. Next, pour over the cheese sauce and scatter the top with grated Parmesan. Place the dish on the middle shelf of the oven and bake for about 10–15 minutes, or until it is bubbling and golden brown.

MAR 11TH

Turkey or chicken escalopes with creamy mushroom sauce

INGREDIENTS
2 turkey breast steaks or 2 small chicken breasts
1 punnet or 175g (6oz) large button/half open mushrooms, sliced
juice of 1 small or ½ large lemon
1 tsp butter
1 tsp vegetable or sunflower oil
1 small glass of white wine
½ tsp hot paprika
1 small tub crème fraîche
salt and ground black pepper

Beat the turkey breast steaks or chicken breasts flat with a rolling pin – the easiest way to do this is to put each between a sheet of clingfilm.

Put the mushrooms in a small frying pan with the lemon juice and butter and cook gently, stirring them every now and again.

In a large frying pan, heat a little oil and add the escalopes. To the cooked mushrooms, add the wine, paprika, crème fraîche and season with salt and pepper, mixing well. Turn the escalopes over after about 2 minutes of cooking and tip in the mushrooms. Stir and allow to bubble gently for a further 3–4 minutes until the turkey or chicken is cooked thoroughly and the juices run clear. Serve with plain basmati or wholegrain rice and glazed carrots or broccoli.

Glazed carrots

INGREDIENTS
1 bunch of carrots
30g (1oz) butter
a pinch of salt
½ tsp granulated or caster sugar
fresh parsley, chopped

If the carrots are large, cut in half lengthways or cut into slices on the diagonal and put into a shallow pan with the butter salt, sugar and a little cold water. Bring to the boil, then reduce the heat and simmer gently, uncovered, until most of the moisture has evaporated, the carrots are cooked and have a lovely glaze. Either serve straightaway with a sprinkle of chopped parsley, or put to one side to reheat later as they will taste fine.

below: *The best carrots I have ever grown*

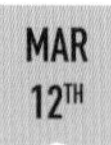

These ribs are so easy to cook and are finger lickin' good.

Scrumptious spare ribs

INGREDIENTS

- 2 garlic cloves, crushed
- 2 medium or 1 large onion, finely sliced
- 1 cup tomato ketchup (see page 89)
- ½ cup soy sauce
- 1 tbsp demerara sugar
- juice of 1 lemon
- good splash (1 tbsp) of Worcestershire sauce
- 1 tbsp wine or cider vinegar
- freshly ground black pepper
- dried chilli flakes, if you like
- enough outdoor-reared lean pork spare ribs for 4 people

Preheat the oven to 200°C (180°C fan) mark 6. Put all the ingredients, except the ribs, into a shallow roasting dish and mix well. Add the ribs and cover them using your hands (wear clean rubber gloves if you have added chilli) with the sauce. These can be kept in the fridge until later or cooked straightaway on the middle shelf of the oven. Baste with the juices from time to time, turning the ribs so that the underneath gets some colour. They will take at least 1 hour to cook through and the juices will all but have evaporated and you are left with a wonderful sticky goo. If you want a more liquid sauce, simply add a little boiling water and stir. Serve with new potatoes or plain boiled rice, a salad or any green vegetable.

right: *The main ingredients*

Sorrel is an excellent addition to the vegetable plot. It is hardy and the young leaves give a lemony tang to salad as well as making a very quick sauce for fish.

Sorrel sauce

INGREDIENTS

1 small shallot, very finely sliced or chopped
1 small glass of white wine
1 tbsp white wine vinegar
150ml (¼ pint) double cream
salt and ground black pepper
a handful of fresh sorrel leaves, stripped from the stalks and chopped at the last minute

Sweat the shallot in a saucepan with the white wine and vinegar over a moderate heat for about 3 minutes, or until the shallot is soft and the liquid has reduced by half. Add the cream, bring to the boil, season and stir in the chopped sorrel. After less than a minute remove from the heat and serve immediately.

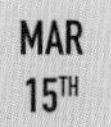

Leek and sorrel soup

INGREDIENTS

2–3 small leeks, very finely sliced
1 garlic clove, crushed
1 carrot, finely chopped
1 potato, peeled and chopped
1 celery stick, finely sliced
2 tsp butter
2½ cups chicken or vegetable stock (water will be fine)
a pinch of dried chilli flakes
a handful of fresh sorrel leaves, stripped from their stalks and chopped

Sweat the leeks, garlic, carrot, potato and celery in the butter over a moderate heat for 5 minutes, then add the stock. Bring to the boil and cook for 10 minutes, or until soft. Add the chilli flakes and sorrel and cook a further 3 minutes. Blitz with a hand-held blender and serve.

top: *Sorrel leaves with mint and chervil*
bottom: *Leek and sorrel soup*

Oeufs à la neige or floating islands

INGREDIENTS

For the meringue:
2 egg whites
3oz (45g) caster sugar

For the caramel:
2 tbsp caster sugar
1 tbsp water

For the custard:
2 egg yokes
425ml (¾ pint) full fat milk
3 tbsp caster sugar
vanilla extract

right: *Floating islands although I slightly overdid the caramel...*

TIP

If the worst case scenario happens and your custard curdles, pour it immediately into a blender and whizz – this should solve the problem and the custard becomes smooth again.

Heat some water in a frying pan and whisk the egg whites until stiff and fold in the sugar. When the water is beginning to bubble spoon the meringue on to the water. Cook for a minute or two – they will swell – and then, using a slotted spoon, carefully turn to cook the other side. After another minute or two, lift out and keep to one side on a plate until all the meringues are cooked.

For the custard, heat the milk and sugar together in a saucepan. Beat the egg yolks in a heatproof bowl with the vanilla extract and slowly stir in some of the hot milk. Strain through a sieve back into the pan and cook gently until the custard is thick enough to coat the back of the wooden spoon. DO NOT ALLOW TO BOIL or you will end up with scrambled eggs. Pour into a pretty bowl and cover with clingfilm. The custard will thicken further as it cools.

Put the sugar and water into a heavy bottomed pan and heat, stirring until it boils. Then leave to caramelise and remove from the heat when it has turned a lovely golden, toffee colour. Drizzle immediately over the assembled custard and meringues.

It must be served really cold. I like to add a crunch. Sometimes I like to add some lightly toasted, flaked almonds.

Stir-fried medley of kale

INGREDIENTS

- 1 nest of wholewheat egg noodles per person
- vegetable oil
- a good handful or bunch of baby kale leaves stripped from the stalks and sliced
- a handful of fresh sorrel leaves, stripped from the stalks
- several leaves of Swiss chard or 1 small bag of spinach, sliced at the last minute
- a few spring onions, sliced
- 1 tbsp soy sauce
- toasted sesame oil, if you like
- pea shoots (see page 34, if you like)
- a handful of micro salad leaves
- a pinch of dried chilli flakes

Cook the noodles according to the pack instructions.

Heat the wok with a little vegetable oil over a high heat and throw in the vegetables. Stir-fry for a minute or two, then add the soy and the noodles. You may need to add a little water to prevent burning. If you have some, drizzle with a little toasted sesame oil when ready to serve – this adds a lovely, nutty taste and add the pea shoots, salad leaves and chilli flakes.

left: *Medley of kale*

MAR 16TH

Spring soup

INGREDIENTS

2 celery sticks, finely sliced
2 leeks, finely chopped
2 good-sized potatoes, peeled and chopped into small chunks
1 large tsp butter
about 2½ cups chicken stock (fresh, or made from a cube/ concentrated stock)
1 fat bunch of watercress or 2 bags
salt and ground black pepper
1¼ cups milk

Begin by sweating the celery, leeks and potatoes in a large saucepan with the butter over a moderate heat for 5 minutes. Add the stock, bring to the boil, then reduce the heat and simmer until the potatoes are cooked.

Add the watercress, stir and bring back to the boil. Cook for 3 minutes.

Remove from the heat and whizz with a hand-held blender – it doesn't matter if there are still some lumps. Season with salt and pepper, add the milk and blitz quickly again. Serve either straightaway, or the next day. I'm not a huge fan of cold soups, but if you like them it's worth a try – only, it would probably be nicer if you added some single or double cream before serving and a few chopped chives.

right: *Spring soup*

Our forced rhubarb has been brilliant this year and instead of stewing it for pudding I picked enough to turn into jelly.

above: *The rhubarb forcer*

Rhubarb jelly

INGREDIENTS
about 1lb forced rhubarb
juice of 2 oranges
jam sugar with pectin
½ pint (300ml) water

I topped and tailed the sticks, cut them with scissors into 2.5cm (1in) pieces and put them in a large pan with the orange juice and water. I brought it gently to the boil, stirring all the while and when the rhubarb was cooked and beginning to turn to mush, I put it into a jelly bag so that the juices could strain through. I then measured the juice and weighed the same amount of sugar (rhubarb is low in pectin and so use special jam sugar with added pectin).

When I was ready to make the jelly, I put some clean jam jars into a warm oven to sterilise (see page 5) and also put a small metal dish into the freezer. Next, I brought the juice to the boil and boiled it for 5–8 minutes allowing some of the water content to evaporate. I then added the sugar, stirring until it had dissolved and brought it back to a rolling boil until it reached setting point on my jam thermometer (If you have a dish in the freezer, then put a tiny amount on the cold dish. If it wrinkles when you run your finger through it, it is ready).

I poured the jelly into my hot jam jars, sealed and labelled them. This jelly can be kept for up to six months. Once opened, store in the fridge.

My first attempt didn't set therefore I emptied the jelly back into a pan and boiled it for a good 5–8 minutes. Trusting that all would be well, I re-filled the washed jam jars and in 24 hours it had set sufficiently. It was a lovely change from redcurrant jelly.

MAR 18TH

The vegetable garden is in full swing with four different varieties of spuds in the ground under fleece alongside garlic, red onions and shallots also sown. Pudding last night was a nursery treat.

Baked egg custard

INGREDIENTS

- 2 egg yolks or 1 whole egg
- 1¼ cups full fat milk
- 1 tbsp honey
- freshly grated nutmeg
- gingernuts

Preheat the oven to 200°C (180°C fan) mark 6. Beat the eggs in a bowl, then add the milk and honey, mixing well. Strain the mixture through a sieve into a shallow baking dish and sprinkle a little grated nutmeg over the top. Place the dish in a roasting tray or pan, fill halfway up with boiling water and bake in the oven for about 15–20 minutes or until the custard is set.

Still warm, I had a big bowl accompanied by a couple of gingernuts and a meringue made from the leftover egg whites (see page 63) and I slept like a top.

above: *Everything growing in abundance*
right: *Baked egg custard*

above left and right:
Experimenting with straw bales

MAR 23RD

First proper work in the vegetable plot yesterday after what seems an eternity, in glorious sunshine. Last year's experiment using straw bales didn't work out as I had hoped but it did provide me with barrow loads of mulch to spread thickly on the raised beds. The early carrot seeds sown about three weeks ago (protected by a mesh tunnel) have begun to germinate and I have now sown beetroot, kohlrabi and a row of leeks. Today in goes Swiss and rainbow chard seeds, spring onions and another row of carrots. I also planted out more plugs of mixed salad leaves, again protected with cloches. It's so good to be back in saddle.

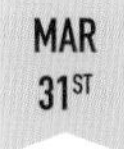

MAR 31ST

A friend came over yesterday to take some plants from the garden and I had time to make something to go with a cuppa.

Spicy lemony cakes

INGREDIENTS

1 egg and equal weight of:
very soft butter
caster sugar
self-raising flour
a pinch of baking powder
finely grated zest of ½ lemon
a good pinch of mixed spice
a good pinch of ground ginger
a few raspberries

Preheat the oven to 200°C (180°C fan) mark 6. Mix everything together, except the rasberries, and half-fill four spaces on a muffin tray. Drop in a couple of raspberries and fill up with the remaining mixture. They were golden brown in 10 minutes and eaten in 3.

APR 1ST

At the last minute a friend over from Houston stayed the night and I wasn't sure what to cook for her as she was still jet lagged. This was really simple to make and went down a treat. Although they say cook the fish from frozen, I let mine thaw first.

Baked haddock with mushrooms and cream sauce

INGREDIENTS

- 2 frozen haddock fillets
- a small amount of white sauce (enough to cover the fish)
- 3–4 medium chestnut mushrooms, sliced
- a little butter
- juice of ½ lemon
- 1 good tbsp flat-leafed parsley, chopped
- a dash of double cream (you can also use single cream or crème fraîche, if you like)
- salt and ground black pepper

FOR THE WHITE SAUCE:

- 2 tbsp plain flour
- 30g (1oz) butter
- 150ml (¼ pint) milk

Preheat the oven to 200°C (180°C fan) mark 6.Place the fillets in a shallow baking dish. To make the white sauce, melt the butter over a medium heat and stir in the flour, then the milk. Gently sweat the mushrooms in a little more butter with the lemon juice for 3–4 minutes over a moderate heat until nearly cooked. Add these to the white sauce, plus the parsley and cream and season well before pouring over the fish. Bake in the oven for about 10–15 minutes until bubbling and brown. I served it with the first Jersey Royal potatoes and carrots cooked with sliced fennel.

below: *Remember when we used to have this strange white stuff?*

APR 3RD

What a difference a day makes: with the plummeting mercury, a bowl of tasty hot soup is called for.

Root vegetable soup

INGREDIENTS

2 large carrots, chopped
2 celery sticks, sliced
1 sweet potato, peeled and chopped
2 medium parsnips, peeled and chopped
1 onion, sliced
a good drizzle of olive oil
2½ cups chicken stock
salt and pepper

Preheat the oven to 200°C (180°C fan) mark 6. Put all the vegetables into a roasting tin, drizzle them with the olive oil and roast in the oven for about 40 minutes, or until thoroughly cooked and just beginning to blacken. Put the vegetables into a saucepan and add the chicken stock and blitz either in a blender or use a hand-held blender. Season with salt and pepper.

APR 4TH

Mac 'n' cheese with a twist

INGREDIENTS

2–3 cups dried macaroni
salt and ground black pepper
1 bunch of asparagus, cut into 2.5cm (1in) pieces
1 corn on the cob, kernals stripped from the cob
30g (1oz) butter
30g (1oz) plain flour
1¼ cups milk
1 cup grated cheese, such as Gruyère, Emmental or Cheddar or a mixture
1 tsp Dijon mustard
freshly grated nutmeg
1 tbsp brown breadcrumbs
a little extra butter

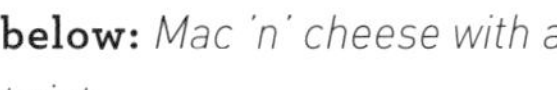

below: *Mac 'n' cheese with a twist*

Preheat the oven to 200°C (180°C fan) mark 6. Cook the pasta in a pan of boiling salted water. In another pan, cook the asparagus and sweetcorn in a little boiling water for 2 minutes, then drain. Melt the butter and stir in the flour in a non-stick saucepan and cook for a minute, then carefully pour in the milk, whisking to avoid lumps. Bring to the boil and add the grated cheese, mustard and a little grated nutmeg. Season to taste. Add the asparagus and sweetcorn, then pour into a medium shallow baking dish and sprinkle over the brown breadcrumbs. Dot with a little butter and bake in the oven until bubbling and brown on top.

APR 6TH

Celebrated a girlfriend's birthday, her daughter-in-law cooking the first course. It was easy, delicate and delicious and she gave me the recipe. Anyone who wants a quick fish dish with a difference, this can be done as easily for one as for 12 people.

Baked salmon with orange and rosemary

INGREDIENTS

1 salmon fillet per person (or whole fillet), skin removed
finely grated zest and juice of 1 orange (or more depending on numbers)
2–3 tbsp olive oil
a few fresh rosemary sprigs
salt and ground black pepper

TIP

Rainbow or sea trout would be an excellent alternative

Preheat the oven to 200°C (180°C fan) mark 6. Place the fish in a shallow baking dish. Blitz the orange juice with the olive oil, rosemary – not too much – and salt and pepper. Pour this over the fish and sprinkle over the grated orange zest. Bake in the oven for 10 minutes, or until cooked. If using a whole fillet it may need to be cooked for slightly longer. Serve with steamed new potatoes – Jerseys if available – and a green salad.

right: *Baked salmon with orange and rosemary*

APR 9TH

When returning with Suzie from a glorious walk in the warm sunshine, I heard one of the chickens celebrating having laid an egg. Perfect timing.

Eggy power breakfast

Heat a little oil in a non-stick frying pan over a moderate heat and fry the vegetables with the chilli flakes and plenty of seasoning for 5 minutes. Pile on to a plate and keep warm while you fry the egg in a little butter until crispy and brown around the edges. Slide on to the vegetables and eat straightaway. It set me up for a busy day in the garden.

INGREDIENTS

vegetable or sunflower oil
a handful of baby spinach
1 baby leek, finely sliced
½ courgette, finely sliced
1 Portobello mushroom, finely sliced
2 leftover cold new potatoes (if you have any, if not boil some in advance), chopped
2–3 spring onions, finely sliced
a pinch of dried chilli flakes
salt and ground black pepper
1 egg
a little butter
salt and pepper

left: *Eggy power breakfast*

APR 11TH *Walking with Suzie this morning, thank goodness in more sunshine, nettles were springing up everywhere and I decided to turn them into soup. I added a few other ingredients together with some foraged baby spinach leaves, which had overwintered in the veg patch and a young garlic bulb. Using rubber gloves, pick enough tips of young nettles to fill a colander stripped from the stalks.*

Spring nettle soup

INGREDIENTS

1 celery stick, finely chopped
1 medium sweet potato, peeled and chopped
1 small onion, finely chopped
1 medium carrot, chopped
a few dried chilli flakes
2–3 handfuls of baby spinach
1 colander of fresh young nettles
a little olive oil
1 vegetable stock cube
salt and ground black pepper (taste first as the stock cube has salt in it – you can buy reduced salt stock cubes)
1¼ cups milk
a drizzle of olive oil or cream to serve

Sweat the celery, potato, onion, carrot and chilli flakes in a little olive oil for 5 minutes over a moderate heat. Add the stock cube and 425ml (¾ pint) boiling water. Stir, cover and simmer for about 15 minutes, or until the vegetables are soft. Add the nettles and spinach, season, stir and cook for a further 5 minutes. Remove from the heat, pour in the milk and blitz in a blender or with a hand-held blender. Serve with a drizzle of olive oil.

TIP

If you are a keen gardener and are house hunting choose the property with nettles growing wild – they love rich soil which means your plants will thrive. Only pick nettles at the beginning of the season when they are young and tender. WEAR GLOVES!

right: *Sping nettle soup*

APR 18TH *The most beautiful spring weather also brought about disaster: the heron made an appearance at first light and dispatched most of our fish, spearing those he couldn't get through the net, leaving them to die. Also, the fox got into the chicken run for the first time in four years and took away Robbo, our beautiful grey maran. We found her half-eaten and half-buried by the beehives. We dug her a proper grave and then checked on the fencing, finding exactly where the fox got in, securing it to prevent further destruction. Down to three girls, I am being given two bantams as a belated birthday present.*

Some weeks ago I sowed broad beans, garlic, lots of mixed lettuces and leeks in the greenhouse – the garlic cloves and beans one to a pot, lettuces and leeks in tiny clusters in modules. The lettuces I shall pick as cut-and-come-again sheltering them with a plastic tunnel. The bean seedlings are now in the ground planted in double rows, the leeks in little clumps, rather than separating them as I should have done. They may not be as fat and white as ones given individual holes made with a dibber, but it was a jolly sight quicker. The garlic is also roaring away.

above: *The fish thief on the prowl*
left: *Purple flowered broad beans*

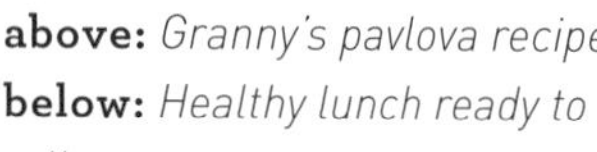
above: *Granny's pavlova recipe*
below: *Healthy lunch ready to roll*

APR 19TH

This is a perfect pudding for Easter. My grandmother Esmé was given this recipe by a Jehovah's Witness in Wanganui during WW2.

All-in-one pavlova

INGREDIENTS

3 egg whites
225g (8oz) caster sugar
3 tsp cornflour
2 tsp vanilla extract
1 tsp white wine or cider vinegar

Preheat the oven to 110°C (90°C fan) mark ¼. Put all the ingredients into a clean bowl with 3 tbsp warm water and whisk until you have glossy stiff peaks. Place a piece of baking parchment on to a baking tray, fixing the corners with a dab of the raw meringue. Pour the mixture on to the parchment and shape into a rough circle, making a slight dip in the middle. Bake in the oven for 1 hour, then remove and allow to cool. Only assemble with whipped cream and the fruit of your choice just before serving or the meringue will go soggy.

APR 21ST

After a wonderful (but a bit chilly in the wind) morning spent in the garden, this was my lunch: baby spinach, micro leaves, baby pak choi, rocket, radishes, lettuce, chives, parsley, mint, egg and sorrel.

I feel squeaky clean. Now I want cake.

APR 24TH

Baked butter beans

INGREDIENTS

1 small bag of spinach or 4–6 chard leaves, stalks included
400g (14oz) can butter beans, drained and rinsed well
2 tomatoes, chopped
a mix of any fresh herbs, such as parsley, basil or chervil
1 garlic clove, crushed
salt and ground black pepper
2 tbsp grated cheese, such as Gruyère or Cheddar
olive oil to drizzle

Preheat the oven to 200°C (180°C fan) mark 6. Wilt the spinach or chard in a pan with a little boiling water for 2 minutes, drain well and lay it on the bottom of a small gratin dish, the butter beans on top, then with the tomatoes. Scatter over the herbs and garlic. Season well with salt and pepper and sprinkle with the grated cheese. Drizzle with a little olive oil and bake in the oven for 10–20 minutes until brown and bubbling.

above: *Inherited from Mama – one of her favourite flowers, a primula auricula*
left: *Baked butter beans*

APR 27TH

Spring vegetable bake

INGREDIENTS

1 standard bag of spinach or 4–6 chard leaves, stalks included
1 bunch of asparagus, trimmed
2 tomatoes, sliced
2 large eggs, lightly beaten
2 heaped tsp plain flour
4 tbsp crème fraîche
salt and ground black pepper
1 tbsp fresh herbs, such as parsley, basil, oregano and/or thyme leaves, chopped
1 heaped cup grated strong cheese (I used a mixture of Parmesan and Gruyére but Cheddar is fine, even mozzarella or feta)

First, I preheated the oven to 200°C (180°C fan) mark 6. I wilted the spinach in a pan with a splash of boiling water for 2 minutes, drained it and chopped it roughly before spreading it on the bottom of the flan. I cut the asparagus into 2.5cm (1in) pieces and added this to the spinach plus the sliced tomatoes.

I beat the eggs with the flour, crème fraîche, seasoning, chopped herbs and the cheese. The thick, cheesy sauce was poured over the vegetables and baked in the oven for 25–30 minutes until it was puffed up and golden brown.

TIP

Against the wall near the rhubarb I found a clump of self-sown chervil, one of my favourite herbs. With a faint hint of aniseed, it is a useful addition to pasta, stews, omelettes, etc.

TIP

I used to grow parsley from seed but it can be tricky to germinate. Now, to save time, I buy a small pot from the supermarket and tease out the seedlings into little clumps, planting them in the raised beds. They look miserable for a few days but soon pick up.

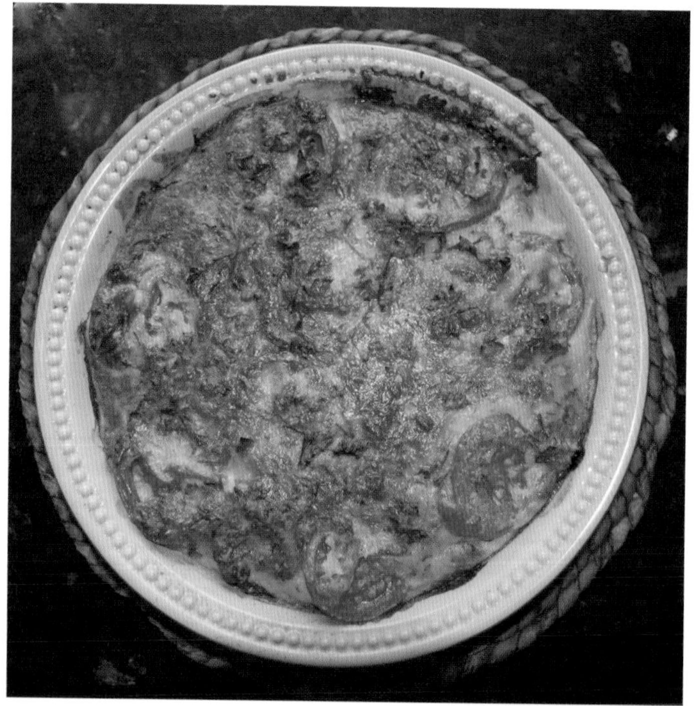

right: *Spring vegetable flan*

APR 30TH Potage du jour

Sweat the vegetables in the butter for a minute or two over a moderate heat, then add the stock or water. Bring to the boil, reduce the heat and simmer for about 10 minutes until everything is soft. Add the milk and blitz in a blender or use a hand-held blender, then season with salt and pepper.

INGREDIENTS

- 1 large leek, finely sliced
- 1 bunch of asparagus, trimmed and cut into small pieces
- 1 large potato, peeled and cut into small chunks
- a little butter
- 2½ cups chicken or vegetable stock or water
- 1 small cup milk
- salt and ground black pepper
- a little butter

Croutons

Preheat the oven to 200°C (180°C fan) mark 6. Mix the bread with the garlic, olive oil and a little salt and spread out on a baking tray. Bake in the oven for 4–5 minutes until golden brown. Watch carefully so that they don't burn. Either use straightaway or store for a few days in a screw-top jar once they are cold. These also make tasty nibbles.

FOR THE CROUTONS

- 2 slices stale bread, crusts removed and cut into cubes
- 1 garlic clove, crushed
- olive oil
- salt

left: *Potage du jour*

MAY 1ST

A frittata is rather like a chunky omelette.

Spring frittata

Turn on the grill. Heat the butter or oil in an ovenproof frying pan and lightly cook the spinach, herbs and asparagus for 5 minutes. Add the potatoes and onion and cook for a further 5–6 minutes. When the vegetables are soft, pour over the beaten eggs, season and cook over a moderate heat without stirring for about 5–6 minutes before popping under the hot grill to puff up and brown. Either eat warm or at room temperature.Serve with a crisp green salad.

TIP

This makes excellent picnic/lunch box food, as it is just as tasty cold as hot.

INGREDIENTS

30g (1oz) butter or 1 tbsp olive oil
1 small bag of baby spinach
a handful of fresh herbs, a mixture of parsley, chives and mint
1 pack or bunch of asparagus tips, cut into small pieces
225g (8oz) new potatoes, precooked or use up leftovers if you have them, cut into chunks
1 red onion, finely chopped
2 eggs per person, lightly beaten
salt and ground black pepper

above: *Today's goodies*
right: *Spring frittata*

MAY 6TH

Sitting quietly in the garden after a busy day, the evening sunshine hit this extraordinary yellow tulip like a laser beam. It reminded me of an entry in my autograph book when I was at school in the Sixties:

RECIPE FOR HAPPINESS

'Tulips in the garden, tulips in the park
But the tulips Bryony likes best
Are the two lips in the dark.'

Oh, those were the days... And yes, honestly, this one is a tulip. I wish I knew which variety.

Watercress and leek soup

INGREDIENTS

1 pint (600ml) chicken stock
2 leeks, finely sliced
1 bag or bunch of watercress, roughly chopped
1¼ cups milk
½ cup crème fraîche or double cream
salt and ground black pepper

Cook the leeks in the stock until soft for about 5 minutes then add the watercress. Cook for a further 5 minutes, add the milk and crème fraîche or cream and blitz in a blender or use a hand-held blender. Season with salt and pepper and enjoy.

above: *Double yellow tulip*
middle: *Cockchafer or maybug*
below: *Watercress and leek soup*

above: *French breakfast radishes*

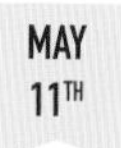

In an attempt to eat as much stuff raw as possible, this was lunch:

Lentil salad

INGREDIENTS

- 1 standard pouch of ready-cooked beluga or Puy lentils
- 1 bunch of radishes, finely sliced
- 4–5 spring onions, sliced
- 1 fennel bulb, finely sliced
- a mix of different coloured peppers, deseeded and finely sliced (½ pepper of each colour should be enough)
- 1 carrot, grated
- 1 crunchy eating apple, skin on and chopped
- about ⅓–½ pack of feta cheese, roughly crumbled
- a handful of fresh herbs you have to hand, such as parsley, basil and mint, chopped

FOR THE DRESSING

- 1 heaped tbsp Greek yogurt
- 1 tbsp sherry vinegar or red wine vinegar
- 1 tbsp olive oil
- juice of ½ lemon
- salt and ground black pepper

I mixed all the ingredients together, including the dressing ingredients. Crunchy and scrumptious there was enough to pack into a pitta tomorrow.

MAY 12TH

We are a grandmother! Actually, no, but the great news is that the intense activity from the blue tits in the bird box with the built-in web cam linked to our television has produced a clutch of eggs (we counted ten) and this week they hatched. The box is fixed to the tree near the sunroom and we can watch the to-ings and fro-ings of the parent blue tits only a few feet away. I love this time of the year with unusual wall-to-wall sunshine almost daily since March. The elderflowers are emerging from their tight clusters so don't miss out on this brief, free harvest and make as much elderflower cordial as you can.

Elderflower cordial

Get a clean plastic bucket (I keep one specially for this) and fill with the sugar syrup, lemons, elderflowers and citric acid. Stir, cover with a cloth and leave in a cool place for 24 hours. Strain through a muslin cloth and put into sterilised bottles (see page 5). I keep mine in the fridge so that it lasts longer. Dilute with fizzy water or, if you want a long alcoholic drink, add some gin, lots of ice and more fizzy water.

TIP

By adding some sliced strawberries and fresh ginger to the elderflower you end up with a truly perfumed, gorgeously coloured cordial.

When Ma and I used to go to Chelsea Flower Show, she froze a bottle of diluted elderflower cordial plus a good measure of gin the night before so that, by the time we were thirsty (usually around 10 a.m.) it had melted sufficiently to provide us with an invigorating noggin.

TIP

I was told once by a friend that, when her horse was troubled by flies she tucked small branches of elderflower leaves into the bridle to deter them.

INGREDIENTS

- sugar syrup made with 1.2 litres (2 pints) water and 1.8kg (4lb) granulated sugar, cooled
- 6 lemons, sliced
- about 20 or so elderflower heads (sniff them first to make sure they smell more of muscat wine rather than tom cat and check they are free from beasties and bugs)
- 55g (2oz) citric acid (this is quite tricky to find now for various reasons but is available at selected chemists)

above: *A variation on the theme*
left: *Elderflower cordial: easy to make, wonderful to drink*

Energising green vegetable soup

INGREDIENTS

- 2 leeks, finely sliced
- 1 celery stick, sliced
- 1 green pepper, deseeded and chopped
- a little butter or oil
- ½ pint (300ml) chicken stock
- fresh sorrel leaves
- 1 standard pack or bunch of watercress, chopped
- ¼ pint (150ml) milk

In a saucepan, sweat the leeks, celery and green pepper in a little butter or oil for 5 minutes over a moderate heat. Add the stock and simmer until nearly soft. During the last 5 minutes of cooking add the sorrel and the watercress. Blitz in a blender or food processor, taste and season and add the milk.

TIP

If done in advance, I think this would make a really lovely chilled soup with a drizzle of cream and a sprinkle of chopped chives.

below: *Energising green soup*

The asparagus is ready to be picked and I wanted to put it into a flan. However, since I am still being careful with the calories, I let my head rule my heart.

bottom left: *Inspirational ingredients*
bottom right: *You looking at me, kid?*

Asparagus and goat's cheese baked custard

INGREDIENTS

- 1 bunch of asparagus, cut into 5cm (2in) pieces
- 2 small, round goat's cheeses
- 3 eggs
- ¾ of a small tub of crème fraîche
- 1 bunch of spring onions, finely sliced
- salt and ground black pepper

Preheat the oven to 200°C (180°C fan) mark 6. Cook the asparagus in a little boiling water for 3 minutes. Drain, rinse under cold water and scatter on the bottom of a medium shallow, buttered or oiled gratin dish. Using your hands, roughly crumble the goat's cheese into lumps, about the size of walnuts, and place randomly on top of the asparagus. Beat the eggs in a bowl, then whisk in the crème fraîche until smooth. Add the spring onions and season with salt and pepper. Pour the mixture over the asparagus and cheese and bake on the middle shelf of the oven for about 30 minutes, or until it has risen and is golden brown and firm to touch. Best eaten at room temperature with a plain green salad.

above: *A small bit of paradise*
below: *Tender little salad leaves packed with flavour*

MAY 20TH *The wildflower meadow is coming into its own and is a billowing sea of frothy white ox-eye daisies punctuated by blue and red from cornflowers and poppies. It is alive with bees, delighted with a running buffet on their doorstep.*

MAY 21ST *In spite of the extraordinary lack of rain for the time of year the vegetable plot is going great guns and, for the first time, I am picking almost slug-free radishes. Way back in February I sowed some mixed salad seeds in modules and, instead of pricking out individual seedlings, I put the whole clumps into the raised beds spacing them about 20cm (8in) apart the result: a successful cut-and-come again crop. I must remember to cover the kale and cabbages with net to protect them from the cabbage white butterflies, which lay their eggs underneath the leaves and cause havoc when they hatch into caterpillars. Ma always said that she never planted anything tender in the garden until 20th May so I have at last put my runner beans, which were taking over the greenhouse, at the base of the canes. Fingers crossed that Jack Frost is now on his holidays.*

MAY 22ND *After a busy afternoon in the garden earthing up the potatoes and planting out courgettes, patty pans, lettuce and cucumber seedlings I cooked the first baby artichokes.*

Braised artichokes

INGREDIENTS

4 small artichokes
½ cup olive oil
juice of 1 lemon
1 glass of white wine
salt and ground black pepper
fresh parsley, chopped

Pick the artichokes when they are no bigger than a cricket ball – the inedible choke in the centre won't have had time to develop. Wash thoroughly – blackfly love them. Trim away the lower leaves from the base by the stalk and cut in half lengthways. Pour the olive oil into a shallow pan along with the lemon juice, wine, a little water and some salt and pepper. Lay the artichokes in the pan, cut side down, cover and gently bring to the boil. After 5 or so minutes remove the lid and allow them to continue cooking until most of the liquid (if not all) has evaporated. Place, cut side up (which will be nicely coloured), on a pretty dish and allow to cool, then scatter with some chopped parsley. The only way to eat these is to hold each half by the stalk and scoop the flesh with your teeth, sucking off the juices.

above: *Statuesque artichoke*
below, left: *Artichokes ready to be cooked*
below, right: *Braised artichokes*

MAY 25TH A very nice duck dish

INGREDIENTS FOR TWO PEOPLE

2 fresh duck legs
2 small shallots, finely sliced
1 mango, peeled, stoned and cut into chunks
200ml (1/3 pint) chicken stock
salt and ground black pepper

Preheat the oven to 200°C (180°C fan) mark 6. Starting with a cold frying pan, brown the duck legs, skin side first. Put to one side. Soften the shallots in the same pan for 3–4 minutes, stirring all the time. Place the duck legs, shallots and mango into a casserole dish, add the chicken stock and season with salt and freshly ground black pepper. Cover with the lid and cook in the oven until tender, about 45 minutes. Serve with anything you fancy.

top: *Baby blue tit about to fledge*
bottom: *Welcome to the world*

MAY 27TH *Since this morning I have been catching the odd five minutes to see the progress of our little blue tit family on the bird cam. There were definitely six of them this morning and now there are only five of whom two appear ready to fledge. When the parents come with food, they peer down at the babies, making as if to fly off, encouraging the chicks to follow.*

If you are growing broad beans now is the time when blackfly strikes, the plants in full flower. One organic way to cure some of the problem is to nip out the fan-shaped, ruffled growing tips before they take hold. If, on your travels up the row, you fall upon a cluster of the pests squash them with your fingers. I had read that broad bean tops are nice to eat, either in a risotto or a soup.

above: *Broad beans in flower*

Broad bean top soup

INGREDIENTS

- 15–30g (½–1oz) butter
- 1 celery stick, finely chopped
- 1 medium onion, finely chopped
- 1 pint measuring jug of broad bean tops
- 1 little gem lettuce, roughly chopped
- 1 large garlic clove, chopped
- 2½ cups chicken stock (I used a stock pot cube plus boiling water)
- a few fresh mint leaves, chopped (about 1 tbsp)
- 1¼ cups milk
- salt and ground black pepper

Melt the butter in a saucepan and sweat the celery and onion over a moderate heat for about 5 minutes, stirring to prevent them burning. Tip in the broad bean tops, lettuce and garlic and stir until everything has wilted. Next, add the stock, stir again, bring to the boil then simmer until the vegetables are cooked, about 10–15 minutes. Never overcook vegetables for soup or they will lose their fresh flavours. Remove from the heat and whizz in the pan with a hand-held blender. Add the milk and whizz again. Taste and season accordingly, remembering that commercial chicken stock is already salted.

MAY 28TH

Red onion and goat's cheese tart

INGREDIENTS

- 1 packet fresh, ready rolled, all butter puff pastry
- 1 tbsp olive oil
- 4 large red onions, peeled and sliced
- 1 long, firm goat's cheese
- 10–12 black olives (doesn't matter if they have their stones)
- 1 tbsp chopped parsley and thyme or 1 tsp dried mixed herbs
- salt and pepper
- 1 clove garlic (optional), peeled and chopped finely, or sliced

Preheat the oven to 200°C (180°C fan) mark 6. Grease a baking tray and lay the pastry, trimming where necessary to make a neat shape and prick with a fork.

Heat the olive oil in a frying pan and gently cook the onions until they are soft but not taking on any colour. I like to add a tablespoon or two of water, which will evaporate during the cooking and means you don't have to stand over the pan, stirring all the time. This can take 20 minutes. Allow to cool before spreading over the pastry base. Slice the goat's cheese and break into bits and place on top of the onions. Dot with olives and sprinkle the herbs. Drizzle some olive oil and season well with salt and pepper, and add the crushed garlic now if wanted. Bake for about 20–30 minutes or until the pastry is thoroughly cooked. Eat at room temperature with a green salad.

above: *Spring flowers in full bloom*
right: *Red onion and goat's cheese tart*

MAY 30TH

Oriental stir-fried chicken breast

Marinate the chicken breast in the ginger, garlic and soy for 30 minutes in the fridge.

Heat a little oil in a wok over a high heat and stir-fry the chicken quickly for a minute before adding the pak choi and asparagus and the marinade juices. Add the precooked noodles plus the coriander, a drizzle of sesame oil and the spring onions and cook for about 5 minutes. Make a steaming hot brew of fragrant jasmine tea to complete the picture.

INGREDIENTS

- 1 chicken breast, skin off and cut into small slices
- 1cm (½in) piece fresh root ginger, peeled and grated
- 1 garlic clove, crushed
- 2 or 3 splashes of soy sauce
- vegetable oil
- 1 large or 2 small pak choi, torn into pieces
- 1 bunch of asparagus, cut into 2.5cm (1in) pieces
- 1 nest of rice noodles, cooked according to the pack instructions
- a good handful of fresh coriander, stalks 'n' all, roughly chopped
- toasted sesame oil
- 2 spring onions, finely sliced

above: *Home on the range*
left: *Stir fried chicken breast*

Index

D

E

ABOUT THE AUTHOR

Bryony Hill was born and educated in Sussex and, after a year at Brighton Art College, she lived in France, returning to London in 1975 where, shortly afterwards, she met her future husband, ex-professional footballer and television pundit Jimmy Hill. In 1985 they moved back to her home county where she learned to garden in earnest, the vegetable plot taking priority. There remained one wish and, when she eventually convinced Jimmy that a few chickens had to join the family, their rural idyll was complete. In Grow Happy, Cook Happy, Be Happy *Bryony combines her passion for photography with developing recipes and cooking what she has grown for friends and family.*